LOST IN
THE LONG GRASS

LOST IN
THE LONG GRASS

JOHN BARCLAY

illustrations by Susanna Kendall

foreword by John Woodcock

FAIRFIELD BOOKS

Fairfield Books
17 George's Road, Bath BA1 6EY
Tel 01225-335813

First published 2013

ISBN: 978 0 9568511 3 0

Printed and bound in Great Britain by
CPI Antony Rowe, Bumper's Farm, Chippenham, Wilts

CONTENTS

to Georgie and Theo

The pen-and-ink drawings are the work of Susanna Kendall, who also illustrated John Barclay's previous two books, *The Appeal of the Championship* and *Life beyond the Airing Cupboard*.

The watercolour on the front cover of the book is the work of Renira Barclay, who also painted the cover of *Life beyond the Airing Cupboard*.

The introductory pages, at the start of the chapters, have been written by Stephen Chalke.

The photographs appear by kind permission of the following:
Lady Herries for page 218,
Lord MacLaurin for page 186,
Phoebe Cripps for page 230,
Patrick Eagar for page 212,
Ivan Ponting for pages 70, 122 and 204,
Sussex County Cricket Club for pages 34, 60, 112, 154, 176 and 194,
PA Photos for pages 88, 98, 140 and 162,
Getty Images for pages 10, 48, 130, 146 and 170.

Preface

Believe it or not this is the third book I have written, and for that I am enormously grateful to both Stephen Chalke and Susanna Kendall whose publishing company, Fairfield Books, has printed them. Whilst cricket is the theme, I like to think that each is quite different: *The Appeal of the Championship*, the story of 1981 and a rather extraordinary year for me and Sussex cricket; *Life beyond the Airing Cupboard*, a story more about me and my life in cricket than anything else; and now *Lost in the Long Grass*, which is a series of short stories about people within the cricketing world whom I have found interesting, amusing and sometimes inspiring and who, in the course of time, should not be entirely forgotten. In short they have, for the most part, added colour to the game.

This book, like the other two, is a self-indulgence. I have much enjoyed writing the pieces and trying to capture the essence and flavour of the characters. It has been great fun to work with Stephen Chalke and meet up with him at Stockbridge once a month to discuss the latest sketch. I feel so uplifted and proud that John Woodcock, one of the greatest and most fluent cricket writers of all, has written the foreword to this book and captured so well the atmosphere of its pages. Also a huge thank you to my wife, Renira, who has once again painted a watercolour for the front cover and got the book off to a good start, and I am very grateful to Annabel Jordan for transferring my scrawled manuscript into grown-up and modern form on her computer, to give us all the chance to read the words in greater comfort.

Above all else, I hope you will enjoy reading these stories of people snatched out of the air seemingly at random, but nonetheless who have played an important part in shaping my cricketing life and the lives of many others.

John Barclay

Foreword

Johnny Barclay brings to the 21st century the manners and convictions of a distant, even imaginary past, and, as these sketches show, he has managed to do so without being left behind.

He is, in fact, a man of parts. He would, in all probability, have made a splendid schoolmaster or a charismatic clergyman, though as someone who clocks up quite a mileage during the course of just one of his peripatetic after-dinner speeches, he might have felt uncomfortably confined in a pulpit. Like his distinguished father he would, I am sure, have made a discerning diplomat, and no salmon or trout is safe when he pulls on his waders. Mike Atherton, now an accomplished fly-fisherman, has Johnny to thank for introducing him to the glories of this sport, when one was the captain and the other the assistant manager on an England tour to South Africa.

But rather than teaching or preaching or being 'our man' in wherever, Johnny has given himself to cricket, first for the fun and challenge of playing it and then as a way of enhancing young lives. In the 27 years for which he has been director of cricket and coaching for the Arundel Castle Cricket Foundation he has become a father figure to hundreds, possibly thousands, of under-privileged children who have found their way, however fleetingly, into a world they can never so much have dreamt of.

Johnny would have been in his element playing as an amateur in the 1930s, perhaps even winning an England cap, by taking an MCC side to India or the West Indies, who did not need to be taken quite as seriously then as they do now. As it was, he captained Sussex for six years in the 1980s, by when the amateur was a thing of the past and the game was becoming increasingly competitive. This can't have been easy for someone so affable, who believed that cricket, to be worth playing, had to be fun. Coming up against him for the first time, looking as youthful as he did (and, incidentally, still does), it must have been easy for his more weather-beaten opponents to see him as a soft touch.

But he took Sussex to within a whisker of the County Championship in 1981, his first year as their captain, and in reviewing the 1982 season *Wisden* said, "Once again Johnny Barclay led the side as though thriving on the difficult, complex business of captaincy, setting a sterling example with his zest and enthusiasm. If there were occasional errors of judgement they were made in the worthwhile cause of enterprising cricket." It could be said that Johnny was Sussex's Colin Ingleby-Mackenzie without all the same accessories.

Clearly he enjoys writing, and he does it with a gentle humour and self-deprecating confidence. In that I am one of a 'watch' of cricket-writers he has flushed out of the long grass and treated kindly, perhaps I have an interest to declare. Being the collective noun by which nightingales are known, 'watch' may be the wrong word; in this case a 'synod', but not a 'scoop', of cricket writers might be better.

These are not cricket prints of the kind which the great RC Robertson-Glasgow ('Crusoe') did so brilliantly. They are longer and less flamboyant than that; but they come from the same spring, refreshed by a love of the game and a wish to see the best in those who play it. In an age when publishers of sports books look more and more for what Stephen Chalke calls red meat, we are fortunate to have one, in Stephen himself, who knows the true aficionado is every bit as keen to find something less gamy, a need he continues to supply with an ever-growing library of unexpected, intimate and revealing reads. To these may now be added *Lost in the Long Grass*, whose author's eye for human nature, informed by his cricket experience and access to privilege, probably misses a good deal less than his subjects might have suspected.

John Woodcock

Derek Leslie Underwood

Born: Bromley, Kent, 8 June 1945

86 Tests for England (1966-1982)
297 wickets at an average of 25.83
676 first-class matches (1963-1987)
2,465 wickets at an average of 20.28

Derek Underwood was a left-arm bowler whose 86 Test match appearances, spread across 17 years, remain the most ever played by an England spin bowler. Seventeen times he took five wickets in an innings, with a best of 8/51 against Pakistan at Lord's. His most memorable performance, though, was his 7/50 against Australia at The Oval when he secured a famous England victory in the dying moments of the match.

He made his Kent debut in 1963, at the age of 17, becoming the youngest bowler ever to take 100 first-class wickets in his first season. With 157 wickets in 1966, he is also the last man to take 150 first-class wickets in a season. In the years following the reduction of the County Championship programme in 1969, he took 100 wickets in a season five times, more than any other bowler. No man alive has taken more first-class wickets.

The peak of his Kent career coincided with the best years in the county's history, with 11 trophies won between 1967 and 1978.

Hastings was his favourite ground. He took 9/28 there in 1964, 14 wickets in the match in 1967, and 13 (including 8/9) in 1973. Then in 1984, with a 22-year career yielding him just two 50s with the bat, he scored a century there.

In 2008 he was chosen by Mike Brearley as his successor as President of MCC.

Derek Underwood

It was a quiet, dark evening in February. With a cup of tea on the kitchen table, the dogs in their basket, my wife Renira not yet home and with the Aga giving off enough warmth to make things cosy, it was as peaceful a domestic evening as one could imagine. Then the telephone rang, always a minor intrusion, so I turned down Radio 4's news bulletin and answered it.

"It's Derek Underwood."

We exchanged some general chit-chat and a catch-up of news and actually spoke for quite a while before getting to the point. "Can I do anything to help, Derek?" I asked at last, assuming that possibly Derek might want me to speak at some do which he couldn't manage. "No, no," he said, "I've got something to ask you." I waited agog. In the background I was aware that *The News Quiz* with Sandy Toksvig had just started. "John," he said slightly formally, "I'd like you to succeed me next year as President of the MCC." I was aware of laughter on the radio. "Me," I said, "Good heavens, do you really mean me?" I was absolutely flabbergasted; you could have knocked me down with a feather, as they say. In my confusion I blurted out, "But Derek, I'm not nearly grand enough." By grand, I think I really meant important.

My mind immediately shot back to all the distinguished men who in the past had occupied this position. Great people of the law, commerce and cricket, and show business indeed, and occasionally all of those things together. By contrast I had been a rather ordinary county cricketer, albeit with an extraordinary love of the game and its participants, and yet I was being asked by Derek Underwood, *the* Derek Underwood, one of the great slow(ish) bowlers of all time to succeed him as President of MCC.

Despite my instinctive reticence, minor panic attack and funny feeling in the tummy, my lack of grandeur did not inhibit me. Without even waiting for Renira to return I accepted Derek's astounding and generous invitation. My main reason for having no doubts, and so not wishing to sleep on it or consult anyone, was because the offer came from Derek. I was so flattered that a real, hard-nosed and gritty professional bowler, who had had the measure of me on so many occasions, should have seen something in my style and felt that MCC should have a small dose of this too. It wasn't even as if Derek was a special, close friend – in fact on the field rather the opposite. Perhaps he was being a little apologetic for the ghastly ordeals he had put me through and so felt pity for me. But I doubt it. By the time Renira got home, *The Archers* was just finishing and life was carrying on as usual. "I've got some absolutely extraordinary news to tell you," I said. And then we played a game in which she tried to guess. After we had trudged through most of the family being pregnant or getting married, she gave up. "Oh tell me," she said. So I did. "Well, that'll be nice for you," she said and left it at that. But I could tell she was excited and so was I.

Derek was without doubt an extraordinary bowler, the like of which I have neither encountered nor seen emulated since. For a spinner he had a longish run-up which he always marked out meticulously although, after years and years, he must have known where he ran from. His approach was somewhat flat-footed and ungainly, but it propelled him as if by magic from behind the umpire, left wrist cocked with ball in hand. Then, unlike the classical 'finger' spinners – Laker, Titmus, Illingworth, Edmonds – he had a surprisingly long bowling stride, more like that of a seam bowler. So much so that it was not unknown for him to bowl the occasional no-ball. His front foot landed wide bisecting the popping and return creases where he would dig quite a hole during a long spell.

The thing about Derek was that he was very strong. He had to be. He bowled such long spells with an action that was full of energy and effort. Standing taller than you might think at just over six foot, he must have had a back made of steel and very powerful legs to make up for his lack of athleticism. And then that combination of wrist and fingers which was able to extract something from even the most benign of pitches. Very few batsmen, often in the most placid conditions, ever got after him. Underwood even held his own in that famous Test match at The Oval against the West Indies in 1976 when Viv Richards played possibly his finest ever Test innings. Kepler Wessels might have got hold of him once at

Tunbridge Wells for a couple of overs but I'm not even really sure of that. Memory slightly fails me.

Not only was Underwood physically and technically strong, he was also rock solid in the mind. He didn't appear to be fazed by anything – always calm, composed and measured. Outwardly he wasn't as demonstrative as some – no cursing or swearing – but inwardly he was fiercely competitive, much more so than his countenance would suggest, and he hated conceding runs. By contrast, Norman Gifford, the only spinner I can think of who came remotely close to challenging Underwood, would growl a lot and display his aggression rather more overtly. Two very different characters and both experts at their craft.

So absorbed was Underwood in his bowling that he never liked to set his own field; he preferred to leave that to his captains: Cowdrey (Colin), Denness, Tavaré and Cowdrey (Chris). When he bowled a bad ball which was rare, he would simply sweep his left hand in front of him as if to say 'Dash it' and then get on with the next one.

*

I first encountered Underwood when as a 19-year-old I was selected to play Sussex's opening match of 1973, against Kent on the famous old Central ground at Hastings. It was early May; the weather was cheerless and cold, the pitch firm and green. Kent batted first and proceeded serenely enough, if unexcitingly, for 112 overs before declaring at 282 for five. My own bowling was treated with the same kindly respect as the others, and I was thrilled to take the wickets of Graham Johnson and Colin Cowdrey.

Heavy rain overnight had soaked the pitch which was left open to the elements. The start was delayed until after lunch by which time the sun had emerged from the clouds and Underwood was soon brought on to bowl. A remarkable feature of the man is that he had hardly ever been known to fail in such conditions. Day in, day out, he was the best 'stock' bowler in the country but, given a wet or dusty pitch, he became a ruthless killer. "Chuck the ball to 'Deadly', and he will bowl them out." And this he did with neither fuss nor flamboyance as if the outcome was predestined. Behind his mild facade Underwood was as tough as any on the field of battle.

In favourable bowling conditions he appeared to be infallible. Many batsmen resigned themselves to failure before they had even reached the crease. I fear that I probably came into that category. With the Sussex score 57 for six, I walked timidly from the old Hastings pavilion to face the bowling. John Spencer had been bowling spinners to me in the dressing-room prior to this, and I had been conscientiously practising my forward defensive shot. I took guard surrounded by expectant fielders in Kent caps (no sign of a helmet then).

I awaited my first ball from Underwood. Not as slow as I expected, I thrust out my pad and bat in an attempt to smother the spin, only to be struck painfully on the end of my right thumb whence the ball ballooned up gently to Cowdrey fielding at second slip where he caught the catch. There was no great ceremony or celebration; it wasn't a big wicket for them and the Kent team took it in their stride as part of the natural course of events. There may just have been a "Well bowled, Derek" and a modest hand-shake but not much more. Fifteen minutes later we were all out for 67, and that was the end of play for the day.

I spent a restless night agonising over the prospect of making a pair – a nought in each innings – indeed possibly a king pair in my case – two first-ballers. I hardly slept all night, jumping out of bed from time to time to practise my batting. A nudge to leg might do the trick or an out-and-out slog, a cultured drive perhaps; I'm not sure I didn't even consider batting left handed at one stage. It was agony; I was in mental turmoil and all caused by Underwood who outwardly didn't look as if he ever wished to harm even a persistent wasp.

Arrival at Hastings the next day lifted my spirits. The ground was awash and parts of it severely flooded. Pools of water had come together to form little ponds all over the outfield, and the pitch itself was surely too wet for cricket to be considered. The Sussex team stood about in little groups, looking on forlornly, while several of the Kent team rolled up their trousers, removed shoes and socks and began to sweep the water off the ground. Indeed the local fire brigade, Kent men I assume, arrived to suck gallons of water from

the field. To make matters even worse the storm clouds receded and the sun emerged. By four o'clock the two umpires, Bill Alley and Ken Palmer, both from Somerset and so well used to conditions such as this, deemed the ground was fit to play.

In the Sussex team there was a lot of talk about not being able to do worse than yesterday, but we comfortably managed it, being bowled out for 54 in 20 overs. After intense instruction and coaching from Spencer, I trudged out to bat at 26 for six, shaking with anxiety and terrorised by the phalanx of close fielders. Underwood's first ball to me was very fast, a real fizzer which some years later, due to the Falklands conflict, came to be known as his exocet. Anyway it hit my bat very hard and flew off along the ground backward of square on the leg side. I turned just in time to see Luckhurst at leg slip stick out his left hand and make a brilliant stop. Maddening, but I was delivered from the indignity of a king pair if nothing else.

The next ball was slower and had a more flighted trajectory. It hit the ground and spat venomously at me, removing a small piece of turf before rearing up and striking once again my sore right thumb. It arced ominously towards Cowdrey at second slip who took the catch, so disproving the theory that lightning never strikes twice.

On my return to the pavilion John Spencer shook me warmly by the hand and congratulated me for surviving one ball out of three from Underwood in the match.

*

When Underwood asked me to succeed him as President of MCC, it did cross my mind that perhaps he might think he owed me a bit of a favour after traumatising me to such an extent at Hastings all those years ago.

Eleven years after Underwood's bowling triumph at Hastings, we played there again, this time in early July and with rather more sunshine. Far from being a paradise for spin, it was the seam and swing bowlers – Ellison and Alderman for Kent, Le Roux and Colin Wells for Sussex – who did the trick. Only two batsmen mastered the conditions, Colin Wells of Sussex and Derek Underwood for Kent. The match itself was unusual. Kent were bowled out for 92 soon after lunch on the first day. Sussex fared little better, scoring 143 all out before close of play and even leaving time for Kent to begin its second innings.

The most significant of all the wickets to fall on this extraordinary day was the twenty-first as it brought Underwood to the crease as night-watchman. He survived the few balls he had to face, and Kent finished the day on 22 for one. Underwood was both courageous and reliable. I don't know if he ever grumbled about being night-watchman, but I can see him now walking unathletically out to bat late in the evening in Test matches to give the opposition bowlers – Thomson, Lillee, or a quartet of West Indian quicks – target practice before close of play. I suppose helmets, arm and chest guards appeared in the late seventies, but before that it was very much a case of going into battle without armour. Underwood was brave and didn't fuss. He just got on with it. Indeed as MCC President he stamped his mark on the position by just being Derek Underwood, legendary slow left-arm bowler and man of great charm – except when bowling on a wet wicket. Then he was gritty and uncompromising.

So, on that second day, with wickets tumbling all around him, Underwood stood firm at the crease, determined and resolute. He never really looked like getting out. Kent slumped ominously to 86 for six, only a handful of runs ahead and with all the specialist batsman out. The harder we tried the worse we bowled at Underwood – too many attempted yorkers which he stabbed out and bouncers which he flapped at quite successfully. But not enough of the good length balls that had flummoxed the top order. Why do we so often bowl differently to the tail?

Underwood found an unlikely partner in Alderman, himself an outstandingly bad batsman who only batted number ten because following him was Kevin Jarvis, comfortably the worst batsman in the world so far as I could see. When Underwood had 92 and I was in total despair he edged a ball from Wells to me at second slip and I dropped it – not a hard chance but the sort of thing that happens when things are going badly – perhaps another reason for Underwood to feel kindly disposed towards me. And so he reached his maiden hundred in his 22nd season and 618th first-class innings. It was not one of Sussex's finest hours, but we all shared in his great moment.

The upshot of all this was a quite remarkable cricket match in which Sussex required 193 runs to win with plenty of time available on the final afternoon. Things looked grim at 113 for six but then Wells and Ian Greig began to get to grips with Kent's potent seam attack plus Underwood. At 186 for six and with only seven runs needed for victory, I assume that even Underwood was conceding defeat despite his heroics with the bat, though astonishingly he had only taken one wicket in the match.

At this point Greig tried to hit Ellison over the top but merely lobbed up a catch to mid-off. Le Roux, usually so reliable and level-headed in a crisis, limply pushed forward to Ellison and edged to slip, out first ball. All of a sudden, seven runs needed and only two wickets in hand. Panic set in. Wells hit a four but was then caught at slip off Alderman. Young David Smith, deputising for Ian Gould, and Chris Waller scrambled a run each to bring the scores level. Surely a final run could be squeezed from somewhere. But no, the curtain came down on this remarkable encounter when Smith propped forward, as many had done before, to Alderman and was neatly caught by Tavaré at slip. The match was tied, a feature that was quickly forgotten, but Underwood's hundred would be remembered for ever, especially by Underwood himself.

*

To my way of thinking, only Tony Greig came close to thwarting Underwood the bowler. On a rain-affected pitch at Hove in the mid-seventies, Greig took an off-stump guard, stood tall and upright and succeeded in disrupting Underwood's usual dominance by attempting to play into, rather than with, the spin of the ball. He made a fine defensive century which demonstrated both commitment and self-belief, even if it didn't save the game. Just for a moment it showed to us young players that perhaps in such conditions Underwood was not totally unplayable.

Underwood had a lot of time for Greig and had witnessed his infectious style of leadership both in England and abroad. It was Greig who was prepared to crouch low down at silly-point ready to take catches almost off the face of the bat. Indian crowds in particular loved Greig's enthusiasm, and he rarely disappointed them in return. It was therefore no surprise that Underwood along with others was willing to sign up to Kerry Packer's World Series cricket in 1977 with the prospect of earning more money by far than he had hitherto done from his international career. In business terms it was a very natural and tempting career move.

Underwood followed his leader, taking to Australia an abundance of self-confidence though not a trace of arrogance. Nothing changed. He performed in exactly the same way, mean and determined as a bowler but generous off the field.

When the Queen visited Lord's in 2009, Underwood as MCC President was responsible for hosting the event and looking after Her Majesty. Rarely can a Royal visit have been more relaxed and enjoyed than this one; indeed the Queen lingered at Lord's with Prince Philip for a good half-hour longer than was expected. Underwood mastered this visit with the same calm assurance that he put into his bowling.

He thrived on pressure and rarely, if ever, failed to rise to the occasion.

Geoffrey Miller

Born: Chesterfield, Derbyshire, 8 September 1952

34 Tests for England (1976-1984)
1,213 runs at an average of 25.80
60 wickets at an average of 30.98

383 first-class matches (1973-1990)
12,027 runs at an average of 26.49, 2 centuries
888 wickets at an average of 27.98

Geoff Miller was an all-round cricketer whose off-break bowling and reliable batting earned him 34 Test caps, spread over nine English summers and six overseas tours. His greatest success came in Australia, not traditionally a happy hunting ground for English off-spinners. In 1978/79, when a Packer-depleted Australian team was defeated 5-1, he topped the Test averages with 23 wickets at 15.04 as well as contributing 264 runs with the bat. Four years later he had further success, most memorably with the slip catch that clinched a three-run England victory at Melbourne.

He captained Derbyshire from 1979 to 1981. His best season for the county was in 1984, when in championship matches alone he passed 800 runs and 80 wickets, the only English cricketer to achieve this 'mini-double' in the past 40 years.

A highly popular after-dinner speaker, he was appointed an England selector in 2000, becoming the first holder of the new position of National Selector in January 2008. In his five years in this role he has overseen victories, both home and away, over Australia.

Geoff Miller

My first encounter with Geoff Miller came in 1970. The occasion was the annual fixture between the English Schools Cricket Association (ESCA) and the Public Schools at Lord's. It is a fixture which exists no longer as class divisions have narrowed over the years and all backgrounds become better accommodated within the game.

It was a big occasion for young players. No crowd was evident, no need for that at Lord's – just a few nervous parents and agitated schoolmasters pottering around in tweed jackets and blazers with newspapers tucked beneath their arms. It meant so much to me, too much really. I warmed up and loosened my joints in the nets after the drive up from Sussex. I didn't feel good – a twinge in the back, fingers not working properly on the ball – nerves and, if the truth be really known, I didn't much want to play. I was in a blue funk.

I confided in my captain, Charlie Rowe, who went on later to play with distinction for Kent and Glamorgan. "You're playing," he said. "You're all right, get on with it." So that was that.

We, the Public Schools, fielded first on what seemed to be a sound pitch down towards the Tavern. It wasn't long before Charlie asked me to bowl, threw me the ball and wished me luck. I proceeded to bowl my off-breaks from the Pavilion end, with a little help from the slope maybe but a short leg-side boundary to worry about.

I slipped into a rhythm, into a world of my own in which the mechanics of the body worked without thinking, and I just bowled. A run or two conceded here and there, it was a sunny day, and then wickets, one after another. Not a procession but every now and then. Clinton and Bairstow fell to balls that went straight on (with the arm, as they say) – my stock ball. Spin was my surprise weapon.

I had already taken all four wickets when Miller came in to bat at number six. He had to worry about neither spin nor drift but succumbed meekly to a low full toss which he obligingly hit straight back to me. Out first ball for nought. "What a friendly chap," I thought. He sloped back to the pavilion, no doubt feeling miserable, and his parents too must have felt the pain, having made the long journey down from Chesterfield. Happiness and anguish sit close together in life's strange order of things.

Believe it or not, I had taken all nine wickets when the declaration came. Keith Jones, the ESCA captain, was mindful to give his bowlers a decent stint before tea, and in order to do this he couldn't delay his declaration any longer. I did get to bowl several balls at the number eleven batsman, though, but to no avail.

Little could I have imagined that day, as I enjoyed the triumph of taking wickets at Lord's, how often I would cross paths with the ESCA number six who had come and gone in one ball – and how in time he would reach much greater heights than me within the game.

*

Later that same year I was selected to tour India with the English Schools Cricket Association, amongst a squad of 15 players that included Graeme Clinton, Charlie Rowe, Alan Butcher and Geoff Miller. This was a major adventure into unknown territory. Our plane was delayed at Heathrow due to engine trouble; we spent more than twelve hours hanging about restlessly and uncomfortably in the terminal building.

Weary and jet-lagged we finally landed in the early morning in Delhi. We had missed our connection to Amritsar where we were due to play on the following day against North Zone in the first of ten three-day matches which would include five 'Tests' against All-India Schools.

Dressed in blazers and ties, we were greeted by Indian officials, garlands of flowers and red dots pressed upon our foreheads as we were ushered out into the dawn smog of Delhi which was waking up for a new day. It was cold. Shivering, ill at ease and uncomfortable we were bundled into taxis, four to a car as well as the driver.

The only way of getting to Amritsar for the start of the match was to drive the 250 miles north from Delhi. The journey was bumpy and cramped. With three of us crammed into the back, we took it in turns to travel in the front seat and talk to the driver. If nothing else it was a fine way to get our first glimpse of this extraordinary country as we rattled out of the Delhi suburbs and eventually into the countryside and through villages busy with daily activity. It was an eye-opener that was as much a part of our education as any cricket would be. From time to time we stopped in the villages for refreshment – sweet tea and Coca Cola mainly. We stood in little groups by the side of the dusty road, pale-faced and tired, staring around us at scenes of apparent chaos and squalor.

In the early evening we arrived in Amritsar and found our hotel in the town's busy square. It was very noisy and smelt of spices. We were greeted by the owners with more sweet tea and some biscuits. Our minds were numbed and our balance somewhat out of kilter which tends to be the case after a long journey.

Despite the jet lag we all woke early, the combination of nerves and excitement before our first match. It was a cold and misty morning. There was a heavy dew on the grass visible from our bus which drew up behind the pavilion. On the cricket square there were two large oxen pulling a heavy roller across the pitch, both flattening the surface and squeezing out the last remnants of dew. With legs still shaking from anticipation and shaky from the long journey, we won the toss and batted first.

For a while all went well. Jimmy Foat from Millfield School and Gloucestershire batted impressively all morning. But after lunch – curry, rice and fruit – there was a collapse. When the fifth wicket fell I walked, trembling, out to bat. The opposition captain, Praveen Oberoi, reputed to be from a very wealthy Punjabi family, was bowling slow left-arm spin with a most unusual action. To be blunt, he was a chucker with a distinct kink in his left arm. The resulting trajectory was most deceptive. I survived my first ball beneath the clear blue north Indian sky, but to the second I pushed forward shyly and edged it to slip who safely pouched the catch amidst much jubilation. Miller showed good teamwork by following me back to the pavilion shortly afterwards and the English innings did not last much longer, Oberoi leading his team off the field with outstanding figures and to much applause.

Miller and I bowled most of the time on this tour and usually in harness at opposite ends, trying to weave a web of uncertainty amongst the Indian batsmen. That Miller spun the ball more fiercely than I did was a source of constant irritation to me. But there it was. I relied mainly on variations of flight and the 'arm' ball for my wickets, as Miller would frequently remind me. I liked to think I bowled more accurately, but what was indisputable was that the Miller/Barclay combination lulled the opposition into a trance. Unlike most batsman ever since, they didn't dare play any attacking shots and so we bowled better and better and whittled our way through their batting.

I tried to bowl like Lance Gibbs but without the spin while Geoff was perhaps more akin to David Allen of Gloucestershire. His technique and body action were stronger than mine and with a bit more zip and power.

We put up a stronger show in our second innings but, still, the prospects of a pair had to be addressed. True to expectation, Oberoi was well into his spell when I came in to bat again. Fielders clustered around me and crouched low for my first ball. My legs shook just as they did when I stood some years later at the altar awaiting my bride. The ball I received from the slow left-armer was so fast that I failed to pick it up. It careered into my off-stump with such velocity that it shot up and hit the poor wicket-keeper on the chin. Celebration was tempered somewhat by anxiety for the keeper who, bloodstained, joined me in my departure from the ground but this was of no great comfort. I had bagged a pair in my first ever match overseas.

The final day was even more dramatic as we tried to bowl out the Indians in the last innings of the match. The crowd built up throughout the day – a holiday – to around 10,000. With not a cloud to be seen and a hot sun, Miller and I did most of the bowling and gradually, with runs to play with, we ground down the Indian batting. We both bowled well but Geoff undeniably spun the ball more than I did and bowled a good floater. I stood at slip enviously but also full of hope that I might take a catch.

When the score reached 129 for nine and with one over of the match remaining, there was a dramatic turn of events. The crowd, which had become increasingly restless throughout the afternoon and evening, particularly as defeat for the Indians became a distinct possibility, invaded the field. We sprinted back to the pavilion; the stout umpire struggled a bit on his feet but remained unperturbed, being used to such moments of exuberance. Jimmy Foat was tackled from behind and bit the dust; Miller was struck on the back of the head by a stone and complained it had drawn blood.

Back in the safety of the pavilion, our refuge, we were all rather shocked but at least had time to draw breath while the field was cleared. There was talk of abandoning the match but I was quite determined we should bowl the final six balls and so press home our advantage. Back onto the field we went with the evening light now rapidly failing. I prepared to bowl the final over with the crowd held at bay by officials with truncheons. The first five balls were played away safely and each defensive shot was greeted by exultant cheers of joy. The final delivery, a quicker ball, struck the batsman on the pad. The entire English team appealed, arms aloft; it was close, very close. But the umpire, not inexperienced in such matters and fearing for his future and reputation, wisely shook his head and said not out. After another, but this time more friendly, pitch invasion we made our way from the field amidst scenes of unconfined happiness. The umpire had made a very good decision.

From the ground we had to hurry to the station with all our kit and equipment to catch the night sleeper to Delhi. It was a mad scramble and, without food to sustain us, our mood as we boarded the train and found our bunks could only be described as tetchy. On board it was rather stuffy and very hard to sleep. I half-opened a small window beside me to let in some air and by morning, after a miserable night of fitful sleep, we awoke with soot from the steam engine in eyes, nose, hair and throat. We must have looked a sight when we stepped out onto the platform at the station in Delhi.

*

After matches on the Test match grounds in Delhi, Bombay (the Brabourne Stadium) and then at Poona, we travelled on to

Ahmedabad where yet another match was drawn. Miller and I did much of the bowling again on grey, elephant-coloured, firm pitches but I suppose, if we're truthful, we just lacked that final bite of penetration and so didn't finish things off with the killer touch. After Ahmedabad there was a lull in the proceedings, caused by an Indian Airlines strike, not uncommon, which made our itinerary unsustainable.

Our match at Indore was cancelled, and instead we were re-routed via Bombay to Calcutta by train, a three-day journey across the Indian plains. This was nothing if not an adventure and gave us some rest from the cricket and an opportunity to see India from a railway carriage. We travelled in compartments of four and set off from Bombay on Christmas Eve, due in Calcutta on Boxing Day evening.

I didn't travel with Miller. He was inclined to tell jokes which, in his North Country accent, required too much concentration. Also Geoff was much more one of the lads than me. He was very much one for singing at the back of the bus – non-stop banter – while I would sit at the front humming Mozart and Bach and trying to stave off travel sickness. Miller was the life and soul of the party while I tended to curl up in a corner. We were very different.

No, I settled down with Charlie Rowe, Jan Kuyper (South African) and John Carter from Sussex. For three days over Christmas we ate omelettes, oranges and bananas. I'm ashamed to say that boredom caused us to behave badly from time to time when we threw orange peel and banana skins out of the window, occasionally aiming them at men working on the line. In this way we spent a happy and memorable Christmas which resembled, perhaps more closely than usual, the arrival of our Lord in Bethlehem. I think we sang some carols on a station, though I may have made that up, and I spent most of the time reading Agatha Christie thrillers with Poirot and Miss Marple as my companions. As is often the case with touring teams in India, there was much discussion around the success or otherwise of trips to the loo which consisted of a hole in the train floor and foot marks to give you some idea of where to squat and aim.

Eventually on Boxing Day evening we crawled into Calcutta to be greeted at the station by scenes of unimaginable squalor and stench. Traders bustled up and down the noisy platform with goods perched precariously on their heads. Carts laden with booty – bags of flour and corn – were hauled along by thin, emaciated locals going about their business with hungry eyes and scrawny, scantily clad bodies. Beggars crept up on us silently and would thrust their hideously deformed faces and withered limbs in front of our shocked young eyes. Leprosy was rife in Calcutta and now its full effect had to be confronted with a mixture of repulsion, sympathy and hard-heartedness, for Calcutta station was not and probably never has been a place for faint-hearted travellers.

We filed our way silently down the platform breathing in the putrid smell of drains and urine and absorbing an atmosphere where death and life are close companions, onwards through the dust and dirt, eventually reaching our coach which then rattled its way through the crowded streets, over the Howrah Bridge spanning the Hoogly river and onwards to the Great Eastern Hotel whose elegance and serenity could not have contrasted more starkly with the muddle, confusion and energy of Calcutta's teeming pavements.

*

Just eighteen months after our adventures in India Miller and I travelled together with the England Under-19 team to the West Indies where our friendship was sorely tested in Georgetown,

Guyana in a small house we shared with Grahame Clinton. Mosquitoes were the problem, thousands of the little blighters. To shut all the doors and windows made it stiflingly hot and failed to contain the onslaught. It's the singing whine that gets to you, even more than the bites. Despair was setting in.

Eventually we had a slice of luck when Geoff found a spray gun under the sink filled with insect repellent. He and Clinton went mad with this and lost control squirting its contents all over the house and all over me as well. It did not take me long to realise that it was not just mosquitoes that were falling pole-axed to the ground. I too was gasping for air. In desperation I opened the front door and dragged an old armchair out on to the terrace where I spent a night of danger on the streets of Georgetown.

Reluctantly I did forgive my team-mates, and Geoff and I began to form a firm friendship. We constantly laughed about our education at Eton College and Chesterfield Grammar School. Background and upbringing pale into insignificance when faced with a scorching day beneath Bombay's uncompromising sun or a plague of mosquitoes in Georgetown.

For all our differences we had led parallel lives and continued to do so.

*

1976, that very hot summer, was something of a breakthrough for both of us. He took lots of wickets for Derbyshire and as a result was selected to play for England against the immensely powerful West Indies while I received my county cap for Sussex, scoring runs and taking wickets, particularly in the second half of the season. Whilst I was given more opportunity to bat he bowled many more overs than I did. I would always look out for his wickets and runs in the newspapers; up and down the country it was fun to see how everyone else was doing.

Much of Geoff's early success at Derby coincided with the arrival of the South African all-rounder, Eddie Barlow, whose captaincy skills, combined with enthusiasm and energy, gave the county the self-belief and confidence which had for a long time been lacking. Geoff thrived under this new regime. In the same way I was strongly influenced by Tony Greig whose charisma and style matched that of Barlow. But, for all that, Miller in 1977 bowled 655 overs to my 155. I had become more of a batsman who bowled a bit rather than the other way round.

Midway through the 1979 season Geoff succeeded David Steele as captain of Derbyshire but, by the time we met up at the tail end of 1980, I felt he was very low and had lost some of his bounce and humour. He clearly wasn't enjoying captaincy. His game was suffering, and both runs and wickets came in short supply. He bowled faster and flatter. His natural exuberance had gone and negative thoughts were beginning to get in the way. I had been appointed captain of Sussex for the following summer, and he warned me that I would find out soon enough what was in store. The words of a prophet.

By the time I saw him again in 1981 he had handed over to Barry Wood whilst I had only just begun. At the end of that summer, a horrible one for Derbyshire, I remember him sliding heroically on his tummy into the crease at Lord's to complete the winning run for his county in the NatWest Bank final against Northants. A dismal season for Geoff and Derbyshire had ended in a moment of glory. Watching it all on television at home, I was dead chuffed for him. He certainly deserved this triumph.

Geoff's career leapfrogged mine, and his contribution to England was more profound than many realise. He was selected 34 times and was particularly successful in Australia. In more melancholic moments I did from time to time consider that if Geoff had played 34 times for England, maybe even I might have been worth two or three goes. Perhaps I might have played if he hadn't existed: who knows?

From a distinguished international career he is probably most well known for a catch he took at Melbourne. Needing 292 to win the Test match Australia were tottering at 219 for nine. It was surely all over. By stumps on the fourth day Allan Border and Jeff Thomson had, however, nudged the score up to 255 for nine. Both sides must have had an unrestful night. The position seemed hopeless for England when Australia came within four runs

30

of victory. Botham was the bowler and, giving it one last heroic effort, he thundered in and banged the ball down short and wide outside the off stump. Thomson's eyes lit up when he saw this tasty morsel – it was a terrible ball, a long hop inviting the winning hit. Thomson flashed hard and with great vigour, as well he might in the circumstances. The ball caught the outside edge of his bat and flew very fast about head high to Chris Tavaré fielding quite close at second slip. He saw the ball well but its velocity caused it to burst through his hands and away. Just behind Tavaré, Geoff Miller with lightning quick reactions nipped across and caught the ball as it fell gently towards the ground.

Late at night and in the kitchen for fear of waking up my wife, Mary-Lou, I listened to all this drama unfolding on the wireless, just as I had in the dormitory at school when England regained the Ashes under Ray Illingworth, though no sign of any wife then.

So England won the Test match by three runs, even though it didn't prevent Australia from winning the series and regaining the Ashes. It was Miller's moment and a great one, too. He was the man on the spot and with perfect timing. None of this was surprising. He was a sharp cricketer, not a natural athlete but with a keen brain and flair for the game. It is always wise to look out for rebounds in the slips.

*

Both our cricket careers ended unspectacularly, mine at Lord's after an unsuccessful quarter-final match against Middlesex in the Benson and Hedges Cup, Geoff's after a year or two playing for Essex. He must have enjoyed it in the south-east, possibly a little light relief after years in the Midlands.

But, of course, then comes life after cricket, lots of it too and not always easy to fill. We were both lucky. I settled down in Sussex to run a cricketing charity based at Arundel while Geoff, after dabbling with business, turned his considerable talent and wit to after-lunch and dinner speaking. His reputation spread quickly and before long he was booked up the length and breadth of the country.

He made people laugh just as he made me laugh in India. His is a self-deprecating, dead-pan delivery, and he seems equally at home with cricket and non-cricket audiences and particularly the ladies who find his style most endearing. Geoff's ability to deliver an anecdote has become legendary. Indeed, I believe his speaking routines have served to give him enormous confidence which he tempers with a natural humility.

A man of high principles, he is also endowed with a bit of grit. I doubt whether every occasion has been an unqualified success; speaking can be very difficult at times, as well I know. I came to a grinding halt once when confronted in Brighton by the local society of orthodontists. Not one laugh. They hadn't even heard of Viv Richards or Gary Sobers.

His speaking engagements may have tailed off a little but only because some eight years ago he was enlisted by David Graveney to join him as an England selector. It was a good choice. Geoff has always been a conscientious observer and listener, and this in turn has made him a good judge of technique and temperament. When David retired in 2008 Geoff took on the responsibility for selection, with a small team to help him. His relationship with the head coach, Andy Flower, has opened the door for a partnership that shows every sign of flourishing.

Selection has evolved quite considerably as an art over the years. Peter May, Ted Dexter and Ray Illingworth were cricketers of such high profile – all captains of England – that some of their quiet effectiveness as selectors was lost. It must be very hard for great players to maintain a passive rather than an active stance.

Selection should not seek the limelight. Indeed, in times of success the selectors receive and seek no praise and yet in times of failure all hell lets loose. David Graveney changed the mould at the turn of this century and directed affairs with shrewdness and understanding. Geoff has continued in the same vein, kept himself at a discreet distance and for the most part stayed in the background. He has a thicker skin than I would have given him credit for. Perhaps his difficult experiences as captain of Derbyshire toughened his hide. A selector needs that and to have some edge too, without being stubborn or inflexible.

*

I sometimes wonder how our lives would have differed if Geoff had played for Sussex and I for Derbyshire. I daresay he would have scored more runs but possibly taken fewer wickets and the opposite might have been the case for me – more wickets and fewer runs. Captaincy would have been interesting. Minor communication problems for both of us perhaps but before too long I'm sure that both accents and approach would have been understood.

When I was sixteen, I dreamt of being Ted Dexter or maybe Fred Titmus. I wonder who Geoff's heroes were: Fred Titmus as well perhaps or possibly Ray Illingworth. Did anybody dream of being Ray Illingworth? Who knows?

*

In 2010 we met at Lord's in the MCC President's box. England were playing Pakistan. Geoff was there in his capacity as our National Selector, worrying a little about his weight and fitness as well as England's performance. I was busy fulfilling my responsibilities as President of MCC.

I dare say we would have preferred to emulate Fred Titmus and Ted Dexter, but that was not to be. Instead, we looked at each other and agreed we had both come a long way since our first meeting at Lord's forty years earlier.

Anthony William Greig

Born: Queenstown, South Africa, 6 October 1946
Died: Sydney, Australia, 29 December 2012

58 Tests for England (1972-1977)
3,599 runs at an average of 40.43, 8 centuries
141 wickets at an average of 32.20
14 Tests as captain

350 first-class matches (1965-1978)
16,660 runs at an average of 31.19, 26 centuries
856 wickets at an average of 28.85

Tony Greig was the tall, blond-haired, larger-than-life South African who captained England for two years before defecting to the rival World Series Cricket venture of the Australian television mogul Kerry Packer.

The son of a Scottish airman who had been posted to South Africa during the war, Greig was brought to Sussex by his school coach Mike Buss. In his championship debut in 1967, he scored 156 against Lancashire. In 1970 he was selected to play for England against the Rest of the World.

He was a front-foot batsman good enough to score eight Test hundreds, a fine slip fielder and an effective seam bowler. Then, in the Trinidad Test of 1973/74, he surprised the cricket world by switching to off-breaks and, with the extra bounce generated by his great height, took 13 wickets.

In statistical terms – with a Test batting average 25 per cent above that of his bowling – he is the most successful England all-rounder of the post-war era.

After his playing days he remained in Australia, becoming a popular television commentator.

Tony Greig

"Let's be honest," my mother said as I clambered into the car after a morning of cricket nets at Hove in April, "he's like a Greek God." "Who is?" I asked innocently. "Why, that Tony Greig from South Africa, he's going to swell the number of mummies watching their children play cricket in the cold."

Tony Greig was the latest arrival on the Sussex staff, six foot eight inches tall, blond hair and handsome features. His home was Queenstown in the Border region of South Africa. He was discovered there by Michael Buss, Sussex cricketing all-rounder, who was spending his winter coaching at Queens College where Greig was educated. Without doubt he came as a bombshell to the gentle and protected world of Hove and Sussex cricket and in just ten years shook the roots of both the domestic and international game.

Greig, certainly in the early days, neither behaved nor played like a professional. He was far too dashing for that and yet, deep down, he was fiercely ambitious both socially and as a cricketer. That he had a touch of class, charm and style saved him, I'm sure, on many occasions from the wrath of his more measured team-mates. "Oh Greigy," they would say after he had committed some ghastly misdemeanour, and left it at that. Greig, through his dynamic personality, got away with things others might not have done. There was something endearing about him that was clearly irresistible to normally hard-nosed professionals. He arrived with both a smile and energy, and his enthusiasm rubbed off on Sussex. He was a breath of fresh air which in the late 1960s cricket badly needed.

Of course I didn't know him well in those early days. He was too much of a hero to converse with although he was easy to talk to when I plucked up the courage. He liked the young (he was still quite young himself) and, when he later came to captain Sussex, he was keen to fill the team with youngsters – possibly too many all at once – and I was one of the beneficiaries.

Three years before that I was very unexpectedly whisked into his circle, when I got the call-up to make my County Championship debut against Glamorgan in Swansea. Sussex at the time had no spin bowlers to speak of and so I, just 16 years old, was elevated to the first eleven to play with and against my heroes. The St Helens ground at Swansea had sandy soil, positioned as it was just 200 yards from the beach, and the pitch was expected to take spin. It was thought that my presence in the team might just tip the balance. My opposite number playing for Glamorgan was Don Shepherd, a man who, late in the season, was on the threshold of reaching his 100 wickets for the umpteenth time in his illustrious career.

The weather spared me much cricket and certainly gave me no opportunity to bowl. The rain swept horizontally across the ground from the Mumbles on its way to the rest of the country. I spent a long time, all of the first day and a fair portion of the second, waiting to have my turn with the bat. Sussex wickets fell not infrequently and eventually it was my turn to walk down the pavilion's many steps and onto the field to make my entry at number nine, ahead of John Snow and John Spencer. Jim Parks, my captain, hadn't seen me play before.

I took guard nervously from Hugo Yarnold the umpire, a tiny little man peering expectantly over the stumps. "Play," he said and Malcolm Nash began to run in unathletically to bowl. Down the leg side it went and through to Eifion Jones, the wicket keeper who, between balls, began to converse with his brother Alan – in Welsh. It was a horrid moment which threw me a little out of my stride as I wondered what they were saying and what hideous plot they had in store for me. My second ball from Nash was a stinker, the nastiest possible sort of ball. A little slower than the first one, it began its travels outside my off stump but then, late in flight, it curled in at me menacingly as I thrust my left leg blindly forward, whereupon the ball collided with my pad and was accompanied by a large shout from the fielders. Had I been captain or a more senior player I suppose I might have got away with it, but inevitably and with no unnecessary ceremony Yarnold raised his finger to signal my departure. As I walked back to the pavilion I was aware that John Snow was striding like a lion, his considerable mane flapping in the wind, down all those steps. Then I saw him turn and I became aware that, behind me, the Glamorgan team were following me off the field. My dismissal was the sign Parks needed to make his declaration and offer Glamorgan the chance to bat. They batted only for a short time before declaring themselves, thus throwing the ball enticingly back into our court. We took up the challenge and scored quickly given the size of our lead before making a bold declaration ourselves on a tricky pitch much affected by rain.

Now, I don't know how many of you have ever played cricket on the beach, but I certainly have, mostly in Cornwall at Daymer Bay near Padstow. One thing, but an important one, I learnt about beach cricket is that when the sand is moist it is much easier to bat. So when the tide is sliding out, it leaves behind firm sand which encourages the ball to come on to the bat quite pleasingly. The pitch at St Helens was moist and much to the liking of Peter Walker, Brian Davies and Majid Khan who embarked upon the run chase. With the sand well bound together they found little of menace in the pitch or bowling for that matter. The fact that we lost the match by nine wickets was disappointing and, to make matters worse, I pulled a muscle in my leg causing me to limp embarrassingly and to be unable to bowl. In those days there was no twelfth man to rescue a player in such a plight. No, it was awful; you just had to plug away and do your best. I confess I was delighted when the winning run was struck, a chance to conceal myself unobserved and anonymous in the pavilion, surrounded by celebrating Welsh members.

With no twelfth man available, it fell to me as the junior player to make a drinks list for the team and to fetch those drinks from the bar. I was both tired and lame as I ascended flights of stairs to go about my duties and satisfy a gloomy and defeated team sitting downstairs in the dressing room. I assembled the drinks onto a large tray and, balancing it precariously, made my way back through a smoky and beer-smelling bar and downstairs. When I reached the dressing room door it was shut. I gave it a couple of taps with my foot whereupon it was opened by a grim-looking Greig.

I think it was then that I must have missed my footing. I tripped on a pad, lost my balance and tipped the entire tray of drinks into Greig's cricket case. To watch the contents of his case swimming about in a mixture of beer, milk, orange juice and the scorer's whisky was just about as bad as it got in my entire county cricket career. It was two years before I got selected to play again, and during that time I used to think occasionally of Greig's bag and wonder if it had recovered from the smell and the grease of all those drinks – or whether every time he opened it, it reminded him of my inept performance that day.

Greig became Sussex captain in 1973 and, to my surprise, he picked me for the first championship match – against Kent at Hastings. As I have already mentioned, Greig was a champion of the young and, having selected me to play, brought me on to bowl surprisingly early. There was no suggestion of spin to be obtained from the pitch, yet Graham Johnson provided me with my second ever first-class wicket by playing over a flighted yorker. Then Colin Cowdrey startled me further in hitting a half volley straight to Greig at mid-wicket. Mike Denness made a patient hundred, but so far as I was concerned it had been a good day. Two wickets.

The rest of the match was a disaster for Sussex, as I have already described in writing about Derek Underwood. On a pitch made devilish by rain Underwood took 13 wickets, including my two ducks, as we were all out for 67 and 54. *Wisden* records that this must have come as a disappointment for Greig in his first match as captain. Yet even he, for all his optimism, realised that not much could have been done about this one.

I liked Greig and admired his spirit. He had boundless enthusiasm and, although it was early days for me, I felt he was a kindred spirit and one to whom I could relate. Where we differed was that, compared with me, Greig had colossal self-belief. If I am brutally honest, he was not a brilliant cricketer, either batsman or bowler, but he made the best possible use of his abilities. How he got so many wickets, especially in Test matches, is anybody's guess. Of course, he wasn't a bad bowler but he did take wickets with balls that no normal cricketer would expect to succeed with.

Botham, a few years later, had a similar knack and indeed lured me to indiscretion on several occasions. I couldn't resist his bowling, and it seemed that many batsmen could not resist Greig's.

You will remember that in 1974, somewhat out of the blue, at Port of Spain in Trinidad, Greig turned to bowling slow-medium off-spinners in an attempt to disturb West Indies' many left-handed batsmen. It was an audacious thing to do and something of an attempt to emulate Underwood's more seasoned slow left-armers. Of all the cricketers in the world I've known, nobody but Greig could have pulled off this trick and taken 13 West Indian wickets in the match which England won by 36 runs. It was a remarkable feat, completed by a man whose faith in himself never wavered.

Greig was never long out of the limelight. In the first Test match of the same tour, also at Port of Spain, he was responsible for a major diplomatic incident when, off the last ball of the second day, he ran out Alvin Kallicharran in extraordinary circumstances. Kallicharran alone was holding together West Indies' first innings and had scored 142 not out when Julien at the other end played Underwood's final delivery of the day just past Greig fielding close in at silly point which he so often did. Julien immediately turned for the pavilion behind him; Knott pulled up the stumps and several English cricketers also turned for the refuge of the dressing-room at the end of the day's play. Greig, observing that Kallicharran was also making his way to the pavilion and so was technically out of his ground, and aware that 'over' had not been called by umpire Dougie Sang Hue and that the ball was therefore not 'dead', picked the ball up swiftly and hurled down the stumps at the bowler's end. I have a feeling that Underwood, amidst the turmoil, was collecting his sweater from the umpire. Sang Hue had no option other than to answer Greig's appeal by raising his finger to signal Kallicharran's dismissal. It was a baffling moment for all concerned; many of the players on and off the field had missed the incident. The crowd, however, had not and, what with Kallicharran being a favourite and rescuing the team as well, all hell let loose back in the pavilion.

Greig's popularity and standing diminished somewhat. But not for long. Greig's good-natured enthusiasm and exuberance meant no harm and he was after all entitled to have a shy at the stumps. Kallicharran was undoubtedly careless and contributed to the row as much as Greig. I believe that both teams' managements were closeted in the pavilion to sort out the mess and the hurt feelings. After two hours or so the West Indies Board produced a calming statement, "In the interests of cricket generally and this tour in particular, the appeal has been withdrawn, and Kallicharran will resume his innings in the morning." It was quite a to-do. Kallicharran was lucky to get away with it. The prospect of a riot almost certainly came to his rescue. Greig came out of the affair pretty well unscathed and was able to win back his reputation amongst West Indians with his charm, charisma and style of play.

But life wasn't always plain sailing for Greig. Despite his good looks, his alert mind and a sharp eye for business opportunities, he was afflicted in his teens by worrying bouts of epilepsy. Caused – although of course I am no expert – by some sort of congenital faulty wiring in his brain, it was a condition which Greig had to live with and receive medication for throughout his life. You would never believe anything was the matter with him because he was always the picture of good health and, so long as he took the pills, there was most unlikely to be a problem. He would sleep a lot, often spread out uncomfortably in a dressing room during quiet moments or when it was raining, but otherwise his behaviour was far from unusual. In short he overcame this handicap with minimum upset to either himself, his family or colleagues. All the same, I did put my foot in it once and rather let the side down, not to mention Greig.

Prior to our opening Benson and Hedges match against Surrey at The Oval towards the end of April 1976, Greig lent me his car, a very impressive large white Jaguar, to drive up from Hove to London. He, as England captain, had a meeting at Lord's and preferred to travel by train. In the boot he left his overnight bag for me to deliver to the team hotel. In my excitement I drove to the 21st birthday party of my girlfriend Mary-Lou, later to become my wife, and completely forgot about the hotel in central London.

I never even went there, preferring to travel on my own in the Jaguar the next day. Greig, parted from his essential pills, was not surprisingly furious and hurled abuse at me as he hurriedly shaved at The Oval.

I was tipped off about the pills by more knowledgeable team mates who advised me to keep a low profile all day. Fortunately I opened the batting and stayed at the crease for the full 55 overs; that kept me out of the way. Then, believe it or not, I bowled quite well too and received the gold award as man of the match. We lost the game all the same. It hadn't been a great day for Greig. Although he didn't bear grudges and quickly recovered his temper, I learnt my lesson and didn't make the same mistake again.

Of course Greig was destined for greater things for which Sussex cricket and captaincy was just a stepping stone. Matches in which Greig played were rarely dull. He was a natural leader, although from neither a tactical nor technical vantage point. He had a way with people, especially the young; he certainly made me feel good in moments of apprehension. I well remember sitting in the dressing room waiting to face the wrath of Andy Roberts playing for Hampshire. Greig could tell I was very nervous and came over to me with words of encouragement. "Look," he said quite firmly, "you're as good a player of fast bowling as any. That's why you're opening the batting. You're the best man for the job."

He had charisma, and players didn't want to let him down. This was Greig at his best as a leader and it went a long way towards making up for his tactical frailties. Indeed, as captain of England he surrounded himself with wise people – Alan Knott and Keith Fletcher amongst them – who made sure he stayed on the rails for the most part. It wasn't quite the same at Sussex, but from 1974 onwards his appearances became more disjointed as England responsibilities took their toll.

There was a sense of fun about Greig and mischief too. At Worcester in 1975, just prior to the second Test match at Lord's, he tormented and teased us about the mystery player who was about to be introduced to Test cricket for the first time. We spent much of the lunch interval trying to guess who it could be and cast our suggestions into a bag. Nobody came up with David Steele; in fact, we felt there was hope for us all when his name was revealed. The selection was as much a surprise as the outcome was legendary.

Greig often got over-excited by events and would get carried away in his response. By the mid-seventies the West Indies under Clive Lloyd were coming into their prime. Greig was convinced, as indeed he should have been, that they could be beaten; it was just a matter of lowering their spirits and getting them down. Remember he had seen it happen in Trinidad in 1974 when his own off-spinners had unexpectedly wreaked havoc. Why not again in 1976? Greig was determined to crush the West Indies' spirit and natural flair and began to plot their downfall accordingly. It was perhaps unfortunate to use the word 'grovel' in a television interview, but Greig was confident at the time and full of beans; he meant no harm and, in a way, we all knew what he was trying to say. England survived the first two Test matches before being well beaten in the last three. The ferocity and brute force of the West Indies' fast bowlers would have laid waste the plans of the world's greatest leaders. Rather too much was made of Greig's 'grovel' faux pas.

Within just a year the grovel incident paled into insignificance as the world of cricket was thrown into disorder by a thunderbolt emanating from down-under. There had been one or two rumours of discontent, but it was in early May 1977 that the whispering began to gather momentum. The epicentre of this unexpected earthquake was, rather surprisingly, the county ground at Hove where Australia was playing a three-day warm-up match against Sussex. As it turned out, very little cricket was played due to incessant rain, and even storms, sweeping in from the English Channel, an omen of foreboding perhaps. Huddles of players beneath large umbrellas were to be seen littered about the ground with far too much time for speculation on their hands. The world's cricketing press had descended upon Hove, onto the scent of a big story. They followed Greig around like terriers; it made us all feel rather famous. But this was different. An announcement was on the cards soon, and the writers would be shot by their editors if they missed anything. All I know is that, for a young player embarking upon a life in cricket, this was a thrilling weekend spent at the heart of cricketing politics.

It continued to rain and rain. On the Saturday night, by way of compensation as it were, Greig threw a party, marquee and all, at his house in Hove. Food, drink, dancing and general celebration. All the Australians were there, drinking beer out of cans, and the Sussex team and many others besides. No expense spared. Press too were included who, never wishing to miss out on a drink, were given a sneak preview of events to follow.

It was either the next day or the day after that Kerry Packer's revolutionary plans for World Series Cricket were officially announced. Without doubt Greig had been the ringleader and chief recruiting officer, and within a few days or even hours the established order of world cricket, run through the International Cricket Conference, had suffered a knock-out blow to its authority. So far as Packer was concerned, this was a business confrontation revolving around rights to televise cricket through his Channel 9 network. This, for several years, had been denied.

The row simmered and boiled throughout the summer and was discussed not only amongst the hierarchy of cricket management but also in pubs and cricket clubs throughout the land. It even overshadowed a summer of triumph for England who defeated Australia by three matches to nil in the Test series. Although Greig was relieved of the captaincy, succeeded by Brearley, all the players contracted to World Series Cricket were selected on merit, pending the outcome of proceedings in the High Court in the autumn. Greig, despite losing the captaincy, conducted himself well throughout the summer, was selected for all the international matches and proved he had both a clear head and thick skin when confronted by intense criticism and hostility.

I remember being rather excited and flattered about Sussex cricket receiving so much attention – after all, Greig was still something of a hero, to the young certainly. We were all rather on his side and anyway hardly dared to voice an opinion of discontent. Despite the hullaballoo, things, for a while at least, continued as much as they had done before.

I even took some time off from my winter life as a landscape gardener to attend some hours of the trial at the High Court. Sitting up in the gallery in scruffy gardening clothes I was able to observe the key players and barristers at work. My sister's godfather, Christopher Slade, presided as judge and treated the participants with the greatest courtesy. Robert Alexander QC led for Kerry Packer's World Series Cricket and its three individual plaintiffs Tony Grieg, John Snow and Mike Procter, while Michael Kempster QC led for the defendants, the Test and County Cricket Board and the International Cricket Conference. It was great theatre. Greig looked smart as usual in a suit and Snow too, although to see him in a suit came as quite a surprise. They both looked confident. They knew they were going to win.

The judgment in favour of the plaintiffs undoubtedly had wide-reaching reverberations and repercussions for the whole game. Professional cricketers and especially international players have benefited hugely as a result. In due course the management of World Cricket became more streamlined and professional. Greig had taken a big gamble, acted in his own interests as well as those of others and helped pull off a major revolution in the world of cricket management. Coloured clothing, floodlights, an escalation of one-day cricket, a greater emphasis on confrontation, with television calling the shots, were the major side-effects of cricket's new style. Greig championed the cause then and did so ever after from his base in Sydney. I can't imagine that anyone else could have carried this coup off.

One of the more welcome outcomes of this whole upheaval directly affected me and a few other young professional cricketers. The Packer empire was extensive and by way of his widely read magazine, *Women's Weekly*, a summer holiday cricket coaching programme was established in Sydney at Cranbrook School in the eastern suburbs. My team-mate from Sussex, John Spencer, managed and organised this initiative and asked me, amongst others, to come and help. Hundreds of children, aged eight to twelve, were flown and bussed in from all over New South Wales including the Waugh twins who were in fact local to Sydney. Apart from being great fun, ten weeks of an English winter were spent in Australia, all expenses were paid and Packer rewarded us handsomely into the bargain. Indeed, as a result, I was able to put down a deposit on a tiny house in Sussex in which we subsequently lived for five years.

Whatever the rights and wrongs of Greig's involvement and leadership of Packer's World Series Cricket, he will always remain for me, a youngster at the time, something of a hero and one of life's great optimists. For a long time his good looks and natural instinct for public relations and his charm carried him along on the crest of a wave. Even amongst the establishment he was well thought of; Jim Swanton of the *Daily Telegraph* considered him a good example. He was smart too, well dressed and groomed, compared with Brearley who followed him and Atherton much later still. In short he was largely beyond suspicion, and it came as something of a shock for many to learn that he had been busy recruiting players for World Series Cricket while he was still England's captain. But Greig had chosen his way forward. Trust had been broken, and he would argue lucidly that it could have been done no other way.

While Packer's dream began to unfold in Australia, Greig's career with Sussex fizzled out in 1978, rather sadly. After serving an eight-week suspension from the Test and County Cricket Board disciplinary committee, he played just a handful of games but clearly hadn't got the stomach for starting again under new management. So he slid quietly away to his new life in Australia.

We met up again in Sydney when I went over in 1981 to play for Greig's old club, Waverley. I remember Tony and his wife Donna coming round to our flat for drinks one evening. Donna was much taken with our nine-month-old daughter, Georgina, and picked her up enthusiastically for a cuddle. Without warning but with some ceremony Georgie was violently sick down the back of Donna's dress. Not a great moment as they were on their way out to dinner. However, they took it in their stride.

Greig was always a survivor, blessed with the energy and colossal self-belief to bounce back and move on.

Michael Andrew Atherton

Born: Manchester, 23 March 1968

115 Tests for England (1989-2001)
7,728 runs at an average of 37.69, 16 centuries
54 Tests as captain

336 first-class matches (1987-2001)
21,929 runs at an average of 40.83, 54 centuries
268 catches

Michael Atherton was a right-handed opening batsman with immense powers of concentration and determination. A gifted schoolboy and university cricketer, he played for – and captained – England in difficult years, his task not helped by recurrent back problems that forced his retirement at the age of only 33.

As a batsman he could play strokes, scoring one-day hundreds against both Australia and West Indies, but his greatest innings in Test cricket tended to be triumphs of unyielding application, none more so than his unbeaten 185 at Johannesburg in December 1995 when in almost eleven hours of batting he saved a match that had looked irredeemably lost.

In his early playing days he was an effective leg-spinner, taking 45 wickets in 1990 including figures of 5/26 in a Roses match. The bowling exacerbated his back problems, however, and in his last ten years as a professional cricketer he bowled only 28 overs.

After cricket he moved into broadcasting, mainly with Sky television, and journalism, first with the Sunday Telegraph, *then from 2008 as the cricket correspondent of* The Times. *In 2010, at the British Press Awards, he was named the Sports Journalist of the Year.*

Michael Atherton

I am writing this, or at least making a start, whilst on holiday in Kefalonia, a stone's throw from Ithaca, just off the west coast of mainland Greece. This may not have much to do with Atherton but, in exploring the islands, I was reminded of Odysseus' close association with the area. Whether or not Atherton and Odysseus would have had much in common, notwithstanding their separation in time, I don't know. But, from what I can remember from Homer's *Odyssey* (which isn't much), it would seem that Odysseus was both brave and wily and, above all, a survivor. Indeed, he proved it by returning to Penelope on Ithaca after twenty years of adventures. So I wondered, as I lay lazily by the sea, whether some of these worthy attributes could be applied to Atherton. Stubbornness is another one which springs to mind, and I suspect Odysseus would have had his moments with this one, too. Most of us do.

To have success and, without doubt, Atherton has had his fair share, it strikes me that resilience also has its part to play. Greece, now on the cusp of economic collapse, boasts one of the world's great civilisations in the evolution of mankind. Its former glories can hardly now help this country in its present plight, but they do at least say something about Greeks. In 1953 Kefalonia was struck by a catastrophic earthquake, very high on the Richter scale, which killed 600 local people and flattened almost the entire island into rubble. Many of the inhabitants left to build a new life elsewhere, but some 25,000 remained on the island and resolved to rebuild it. This showed a resilient and deeply determined spirit, steely and dogged – adjectives I would attribute to Atherton. Twenty-five years or so later, new towns and villages had been completed. No, Greece surely won't be blown away by its current debt problems any more than Atherton would ever be blown away by a hostile spell from Alan Donald or Curtly Ambrose.

Brave but also wily, Atherton is as much at home casting a fly into a chalk stream as he is with a ball whizzing past his nose. He doesn't like noise. Indeed, he doesn't make much, save the tuneless humming of unrecognisable melodies that signal his approach on the river bank. Michael has become a good fisherman, stealthily stalking fish as a cat might stalk its prey. Nothing sudden or hurried; keen eyes on the lookout for the tell-tale movement of a fish. He plays his golf in much the same way, unflustered and irritatingly competent.

I feel I can at least take some small responsibility for his fishing enthusiasm. It all started after his remarkable match-saving innings of 185 not out in the second Test match against South Africa at the Wanderers Ground in Johannesburg. He batted for nearly 11 hours and partnered both Robin Smith and Jack Russell in one of Test cricket's great defensive recoveries. When it was all over he was, not surprisingly, exhausted, mentally washed out. Immediately after the Test match we flew from the somewhat frantic atmosphere of Johannesburg to the far-away world of the vineyards surrounding Paarl, in the Western Cape. Dutch architecture, wide streets and jacarandas. Peace. We stayed at the Zummerlust Guest House, flowers in every room and quite unlike the run-of-the-mill, city-chain hotels. It was just what was needed before travelling right across South Africa again for the third Test in the humidity of Durban.

"What about a day's fishing?" I flicked the question quite casually to Atherton one evening in the hotel. "It'll do you good."

To my surprise he agreed without any hint of trying to find an excuse to get out of the proposal. Despite the tour being well past its early stages – two Tests played and drawn – I still felt I scarcely knew the captain and was reluctant to intrude upon his space. So we were all set to go. Ray Illingworth, the tour manager, gave his approval and our good friend, Andrew Wingfield Digby, who was also staying in Paarl at the time, joined the party bound for the Worcester valley.

Atherton didn't take kindly to tuition, preferring to get on by himself and simply rely upon trial and error. Although Andrew and I fished a little further upstream we did keep an eye on the England captain who was frequently to be seen submerged in the water, slipping on stones beneath the surface. Strangely, though, and despite these setbacks, he very much took to this new-found hobby. He caught nothing all day but seemed unperturbed; after all, he was well used to batting for a long time without scoring many runs. Clearly fishing suited his character. Possibly it had a similar rhythm to cricket as for much of the time in both sports nothing very much happens. In the evening we returned to the Zummerlust where they cooked our trout (Andrew and I caught four between us) for dinner. The ice was broken. A friendship had been forged.

Some time earlier that same year, 1995, I met Atherton for the first time. It was an unusual occasion and a happy one too. A match had been arranged at Arundel Castle to celebrate the life of Peter May who had died a few months previously. One team representing England and another representing Surrey played against each other on a sunny day in front of a very good crowd. Just for a moment I bumped into Atherton in the marquee; presumably he had got out earlier – not his sort of match really. We just about said hello, but that was it. Of course I had no idea then that I was going to be asked to go to South Africa that winter as Assistant Manager. Our meeting at Arundel might be described as fairly silent, but not unfriendly.

It must have been only a few weeks after the Peter May match that I was invited by John Major, then Prime Minister, to a special sporting breakfast. I arrived early for fear of being late for this important occasion and sat for a while in St James' Park watching the ducks. It was a warm morning with the promise of a hot day ahead and so the party was held in the large garden behind Downing Street. Tucking into rolls, croissants and coffee was a galaxy of stars some of whom I recognised, even if I couldn't put a name to them all. Bobby Charlton was there, that was good enough for me.

The sun was beginning to rise in the sky, shining warmly down into the garden. I was about half way through my second cup of coffee when I was approached by Alan Smith, then Chief Executive of the Test and County Cricket Board, who asked me if I would like to travel as Assistant Manager to Ray Illingworth in South Africa on the forthcoming tour. I was both astounded and flattered. Ray would be manager, Mike Atherton captain and me assistant manager – an unusual mix if ever there was one. The very first time we all met up together was at Heathrow in October when, I remember, everyone was much taken by their new Motorola telephones with our tour colours resplendent on the front.

My first impressions of Atherton were of a quiet man who liked reading books, playing bridge, a little golf and then later fishing – not at all, I would say, your standard England captain. Although he wasn't exactly easy to get to know, I felt he had a comfortable and relaxed relationship with his team. He was tough in the proper sense of the word, not all show and bravado like the Pharisees in the market place. At first I saw him more as a technician and wise advisor than a natural leader. But even if not in the truly ruthless mould (which I think Brearley probably was), he was much respected, well liked and unselfish which made up for a lot in the leadership stakes. I doubt whether Illingworth really understood him well, but they did their best to work together and for much of the tour in South Africa they rubbed along untroubled.

So far as the Test matches were concerned, we only actually lost that last disastrous low-scoring match in Cape Town which cost us the series. Indeed, we could well have won that one too. All the same, it was no mean effort to hold our own as we did against an outstanding South African side, bursting to prove itself in its first series back on home soil under its newly elected President.

Atherton is not perfect. Nobody ever is. He was prone to mulishness, digging his heels in, and so at times inflexible. He certainly had a bit of a blind spot with press and media, quite understandable but mostly more unhelpful than helpful. He hated the concept of 'spin' and public relations jargon. He had no time for it and made his views abundantly clear to journalists for whom he did not care. He never quite understood that he was the shop window for the England team and that his attitude could enhance the cause rather than hinder it. He was, of course, quite young to be made captain of England, but then and even later on he rarely seemed to be aware of the importance of his relationship with the press. He didn't really try. It was a pity, for example, that so many of the South African people perceived him to be dull and dour when it actually couldn't have been much further from the truth.

During the subsequent World Cup campaign in Pakistan, Atherton found himself the victim of a piece of bad luck when he referred to a Pakistan journalist, who was constantly interrupting him and irritating everyone, as a 'buffoon'. The remark which was not noticed at the time was later picked up on a tape recorder and gave the local press the opportunity to take considerable umbrage. In fact, it was one of the rare occasions when Atherton actually smiled during a press conference.

"You can't win with the press if you're losing," was Atherton's view. He was convinced that the only way to keep the press at bay was by winning; otherwise they'd make you out to be a fool whatever. And of course he was right. No sweet and calming words from any beleaguered manager were ever going to quash an editor's thirst for blood. And that was certainly the case during the World Cup when we got blown away by Sri Lanka in Faisalabad before we had ever found a rhythm, let alone a settled team. We were in a muddle, and it hadn't really sorted itself out by the time we embarked upon a short tour of Zimbabwe later the same year.

Atherton himself had struggled with his own fitness and form during the World Cup, and I think his confidence and perhaps even a touch of his steely nature took a bit of a dip. For some years he had suffered acute pain in his lower back, an impediment which he coped with bravely as part of his daily life. But by the time he got to Zimbabwe it had, I think, reached new heights of discomfort. For my money he looked stiff in his stance at the crease, and, maybe I was looking for things, his foot movements seemed more cumbersome and less fluent; he had a pained look in his face. Atherton vehemently disagreed. I expect he felt we were trying to make excuses for him. And then at the height of this drama I remember he took a magnificent diving catch in the gulley and turned to us as if to say, "Not much wrong with me there." But there was. He wasn't fully fit, and the team knew it.

He really should have been resting and recharging the batteries at home, not subjecting his body and mind to undue and unnecessary stress and strain. But he was the world's worst patient and stubborn to boot.

Whether or not it was because of the captain's low spirits, the general mood of the tour seemed to have a depressing effect upon the players. We were supposed to be beating Zimbabwe, relative newcomers to the top flight, yet we were outmanoeuvred wherever we went. We didn't actually lose the Test matches but we were totally outplayed in the one-day games where our performances, albeit against a very able Zimbabwean side (Campbell, two Flowers, Streak and others), were outstandingly bad. David Lloyd, our head coach, despite enormous enthusiasm and a great sense of fun, lost his head somewhat amidst the emotional hullabaloo of Test cricket. He had much to offer but let himself down.

I think it would be fair to say that the squad of players in Zimbabwe was poorly selected, inadequately prepared and shabbily led and managed. Yet, for some unknown reason, when we moved on to New Zealand, we fared a great deal better. I can't imagine why. We were exactly the same group of players plus Dominic Cork who joined the party in Auckland. Possibly, released from the claustrophobic and oppressive atmosphere of Harare in particular, it was something of a breath of fresh air and a new beginning to inhale the sea breeze of islands not totally dissimilar from our own. Without doubt there was a change of atmosphere in New Zealand, a greater degree of confidence amongst the locals and a touch of sympathy too for the way the press had treated us in Zimbabwe, though much of it was well deserved.

We had touched down in Auckland in the early hours with our internal time clocks in disorder and jet lag unsurprisingly beginning to kick in. Many of the team members, including Atherton, decided to forgo a short night's rest and nipped into the late-night bars, still open and serving drinks until morning. I wouldn't say that Atherton was exactly drunk when I met him in the hotel lobby later on, but he looked far from his best – unshaven, unkempt, voice a little slurred and generally good for nothing but a peaceful day in his room. That would have been fine, had it not been for an untimely press conference at midday. To give Atherton his due he put in a determined, stonewalling performance but was forced distinctly onto the back foot by the hostile inquisition of ITN's former war reporter Michael Nicholson, whose belligerent approach would have reduced many to a gibbering wreck. "I've known worse ordeals facing Ambrose," Atherton confided later. It had been a dogged and gritty performance in trying circumstances while still slightly under the influence of alcohol and accompanied by the first onset of hangover, a dry mouth and a headache. I suppose many journalists are used to that all the time.

We got away with it initially in Auckland. The practice facilities at Eden Park were good, and the sessions went well. But still there was the mounting worry of Atherton's form. Cameras followed his every move, never failing to miss an opportunity to show his stumps cart-wheeling in the nets. Perhaps the lowest point of all, and I think there has to be one, was a ten-over (cricket max) novelty game played in a rugby stadium under floodlights and organised by Martin Crowe. I can't really remember the nature of the competition: four teams, I imagine, with a New Zealand entry that included their women's team captain, Emily Drum. Inevitably Atherton didn't last long when he batted, concluding his innings with an elegant lofted off drive which was comfortably taken on the boundary by Drum.

There was much good humour and joy abounding but, for the press, the story was too good to be true. On balance it was not good for Atherton's rehabilitation programme, much as he laughed.

"The tour went on," as Enid Blyton might have headed a new chapter. With the first Test looming and little sign of fluency emerging from the captain's bat we played a match at Hamilton against Northern Districts. Once again Atherton got out early. I came to realise how hard it is for an international player when poor form becomes so public. There is nowhere to hide, nowhere to practise and fret behind closed doors. But then a minor miracle occurred. Behind the pavilion at Hamilton we discovered, and we hadn't known it was there before, an indoor cricket school. It was fairly small and scruffy, no long run-ups for the bowlers and poor lighting – but ideal for our purpose. For the best part of two days Atherton, David Lloyd, John Emburey and one or two other carefully selected players barricaded themselves into these tattered facilities. Gradually, amidst pouring sweat but not quite blood and tears, Atherton's technique and confidence had their chance to regroup. He began to feel a little better and proved it by scoring 12 not out in the second innings, steering us to a ten-wicket victory. It was a minor triumph for him and indeed for England who had yet to shake off the Zimbabwe jinx.

As it turned out the subsequent Test series, despite being thwarted by Astle and Morrison on a remarkable final day at Eden Park in the first match, was a resounding success compared with all that had gone before. Atherton was our leading batsman, and the rubber was won by two matches to nil.

Atherton is an unusual fellow. For a start he's a clever chap. It's no mean feat to come out with a good degree at Cambridge while spending most of the spring and early summer playing cricket at Fenner's. It seems that from an early age he was always associated with captaincy – school, university, not so much Lancashire but then England.

A player of his pedigree and talent is almost bound to end up as captain, yet I never felt that the responsibilities of leadership sat with him as easily as they might, although his players and friends always respected him and certainly admired his attributes as a cricketer. I see him more as a thinker, a man of reflection, rather than someone who will drill a team into action. Atherton is an ideas man, a think tank and a great reader of books but less at home amidst the teamroom banter where so much power can be generated. A great leader, I don't think so. A fine thinker, yes.

Atherton is measured in his approach, sums up the evidence and decides what to do. Not much of a gambler, I should have said. But how wrong I was. Unexpectedly Atherton has been known to have a flutter from time to time, on the horses especially, and not without success. In addition to all that, he has written a book about gambling which must have involved considerable research, scholarship and presumably first-hand practice as well as much dogged determination, Atherton's signature tune. I confess I haven't read the book and don't intend to, but that doesn't quell my admiration for an extraordinary and unlikely piece of work.

Atherton has become a rare specimen: a top class, very good (though not great) cricketer who has taken his honest and trustworthy nature across the boundary into television and journalism. He is a respected commentator on cricket and much else besides.

His honesty is a precious and much treasured attribute and, by that, I don't mean that he will instinctively walk to the pavilion upon edging the ball. No, he won't. We all saw that at Trent Bridge in 1998 when he gloved a ball to Boucher off Donald. Indeed, he is honest about not walking. At Lord's in 1994 he was more naive than anything else over the 'dust in the pocket' incident. I'm not even sure he was really aware that the laws were being broken, but he was undoubtedly more at home with strong referees, Peter Burge and John Reid, than weak ones. Atherton, whose strength is based upon his own integrity, is allergic to spin doctors and the smooth-talking public relations cohorts.

On one thing Atherton and I are fairly well agreed. A successful and happy day's fishing in good company lifts the heart and spirits and paves the way for the fruitful exploitation of our lives. Neither of us is happier than when on a river bank. In Scotland he caught his first salmon, by dubious means admittedly, beneath a footbridge on the River Deveron. This was followed by several expeditions to the Rivers Don and Tweed where gradually his tally of salmon began to rise. One of his early fish was proudly landed and left on a dry brick wall for safety from where it was taken and eaten by Andrew Wingfield Digby's dogs. His best trout was caught on the Hope River, a two-hour drive out from Christchurch in New Zealand. It was a green fluffy fly which did the trick and deceived a fish of over seven pounds. I netted it successfully, much to my relief, fifty yards downstream. Back in my hotel room the England team feasted upon it hungrily.

Now Atherton is a writer and broadcaster. He wears smart suits and shirts with tie knotted neatly at the top button. Scruffy days are now only for private consumption. He is a family man living in Hertfordshire where his two children are making impressive progress at school. His son Josh plays for the Middlesex under-nines, probably under-elevens by the time you read this.

Little fazes Atherton although he did get into a bit of a dither facing Chris Harris' slow-medium bowling for New Zealand. Ambrose was, of course, a handful, but then he was for most. I sense he hates post-Test match presentation ceremonies which conclude many a fine occasion so charmlessly. But otherwise he gets on with things and reads his books. *The Times* is lucky to have both him and Simon Barnes to write about sport and other topics; they are both instructive, immensely readable and funny too.

Hard though it is to look into the future I suspect that Atherton has more to offer this world than merely writing and commentating on cricket. He has greater depth than that. His surprising book on gambling is testimony to that. He's not entirely at home with people, quite a shy man at heart, and yet he has a clear mind which gets to grips with things with neither fuss nor flamboyance. In due course he'll become a good orator too.

I suppose Atherton is essentially one of those maddening chaps who has got it all: sport and brains, combined with a social manner that is more of an acquired taste. And yet not quite all. He has a bad back, and he couldn't play Chris Harris. These are setbacks to be reckoned with and inspire in him a humility which is both a great asset and very endearing.

John Augustine Snow

Born: Peopleton, Worcestershire, 13 August 1941

49 Tests for England (1965-1976)
772 runs at an average of 13.54
202 wickets at an average of 26.66

346 first-class matches (1961-1977)
4,832 runs at an average of 14.17
1,174 wickets at an average of 22.73

Among post-war English fast bowlers John Snow belongs in the first rank, a right-armer capable of generating great pace and hostility from a relatively short run-up. The son of a vicar, he had two volumes of poetry published in the early 1970s. Yet, with a ball in his hand and a Test match arena in which to perform, he was not the gentlest of souls.

His 202 Test wickets came in only 49 matches, his rate of more than four per Test bettered by only Bedser and Trueman among the 13 England quick bowlers to take 200 wickets.

The high point of his career came on Ray Illingworth's tour of Australia in 1970/71. He took 31 wickets, the most by an England bowler in Australia since Harold Larwood on the Bodyline tour of 1932/33. His match-winning seven wickets for 40 runs in the second innings at Sydney, his best Test figures, set England on the path to regaining the Ashes.

His performances for Sussex, once his Test career was established, were more moderate. He called his autobiography Cricket Rebel *and became one of the first to sign up for Kerry Packer's alternative circuit in Australia.*

John Snow

I'm not sure I ever faced Snow's bowling for real, other than occasionally in the nets, pre-season, when he would lope in like a greyhound and bowl gentle off-breaks with a smile of endearment on his face rather than a snarl of aggression.

In 1975 I was 21 and already felt I had known him a long time, but not well. Nobody knew him well. He was, after all, an odd fellow and took a lot of getting used to. We were practising in April in preparation for our annual encounter with the Benson and Hedges Trophy in which we had so far been notably unsuccessful, and I was proud and a little surprised to be selected by the Sussex captain, Tony Greig, to play in our opening fixture against Kent at Canterbury.

The match began most unexpectedly. Snow had obviously warmed up well and unleashed his first over at Brian Luckhurst with startling hostility. I was standing at first slip, hiding myself behind the wicket-keeper, when Snow let loose the third ball of this unlikely over. It was a genuine snorter. Very fast, it veered into the right-handed Luckhurst on a good length and pitched on middle stump. Horrid. But things got worse for the batsman who had presumably wished not to embark upon the new season with such intimidation in the air. As Luckhurst propped forward hopefully, the ball lifted and cut away off the pitch, striking the shoulder of his bat. The Sussex wicket-keeper, Alan Mansell, had been understandably wrong-footed and was steering a course down the leg-side, some way from the action. Meanwhile the ball flew with pace off the outside edge and, with no one else to rely on, I dived high to my left and against all the odds clung on to, though I say it myself, a rather remarkable and improbable catch. I tell this story not so much to boast, although it was a rare moment of success, but more to lay down a marker and point out that in Snow's long and chequered career this was the only time I can remember being remotely helpful to it. In this match Snow bowled 11 overs and took three for 11, adding Denness and Knott to the hapless Luckhurst. It was the best I ever saw him bowl for Sussex.

When I was a boy scurrying around Hove with my autograph book, Snow was something of a hero: not perhaps in the same mould as

Dexter and Parks, but nonetheless fairly heroic and a fast bowler. I first set eyes upon the man in 1963 when Sussex played Worcestershire at Lord's in the first Gillette Cup final. I vaguely remember Snow being bowled out rather dramatically – stumps and bails flying – before, late in the day and in the drizzle, bowling fast from the pavilion end. He made an impact upon the match – and me, too, as I slid away, happy and triumphant, amongst the crowds to catch the bus home.

Only three years later, at the age of 24, Snow was reaching his golden years. Selected for the final three Test matches against the mighty West Indies, he began to have success against some of the world's best players including Gary Sobers, the West Indies captain. At the Lewes Tennis Tournament in August I pottered around with a transistor glued to my ear. The final Test was being played at The Oval, and England for the first time in the series were beginning to get the upper hand when Sobers came in to bat for his second innings.

Snow had already surprised everyone – and himself, too, presumably – by scoring 59 not out in England's first innings, sharing a last wicket stand of 128 with Ken Higgs who made 63. Snow and Higgs were an unlikely combination whether batting or bowling. Snow was moody, exciting and dashing while Higgs was solid, dependable and professional, words that could never have been applied to Snow. Anyway, in came Sobers to bat and only he stood between England and victory. Brian Close was captain, a tough man made of something different from the rest of us, and he set the field, posting himself very close in at short-leg, virtually in Sobers' pocket. Snow rushed in to bowl and, presumably to order, dug in a short one. Sobers went for the hook but was taken by surprise by the extra pace and merely lobbed the ball into Close's hands. This was for me a great piece of fast bowling of thoroughbred virtuosity. Many of us rejoiced amidst the tennis at Lewes.

Snow was in his prime and, by the time he travelled with Colin Cowdrey's MCC team to the West Indies early in 1968, he was bowling at his fastest and best. In just four Test matches he took 27 wickets at an average of 18, taking four or more wickets in an innings on four occasions. Snow thrived upon playing in the Test matches and resting during the island games. He was very much a Test cricketer and not a day-in, day-out bowling hack. England won the series 1-0 due to an unexpected win at Port of Spain when Sobers made a generous declaration, perhaps underestimating England's confidence against spin. The series was concluded in Georgetown, Guyana when Jeff Jones, England's non-batting number eleven, played out the final over, bowled by Lance Gibbs, to clinch the series.

Snow was at his best and most potent on hard pitches baked by overseas sunshine. Where there was bounce he was in his element. Two years after the tour to the West Indies he travelled to Australia to contest the Ashes, this time under the leadership of Ray Illingworth. Snow bowled fast and menacingly throughout the series, taking 31 wickets at an average of 22. Almost single-handedly he laid waste the Australian batting at Sydney in the fourth Test match, returning figures of seven for 40 in 18 overs.

Illingworth, and possibly later on Greig, had the measure of Snow. They understood better than most how he ticked and, above all else, Snow respected them. As bowlers themselves and aware of their strange ways at times, they were more sympathetic towards his moods and tended to pamper him somewhat as a result. Whatever it was, it worked for Illingworth whose side was already a fair one – but with Snow in it there was an added touch of class, that indefinable something extra for which Illingworth must have been hugely grateful.

I well remember listening to the final phase of the last Test match at Sydney in which Australia played themselves into a winning position. My transistor was tucked away beneath the bedclothes of my bed at school. A win for Australia would mean a tied series, a win for England a 2-0 triumph. For a long time the former result looked likely. As it turned out it was Illingworth, Underwood and, perhaps surprisingly, D'Oliveira who stole the honours on the final day. Snow was out of action after breaking a finger when attempting a catch on the boundary and colliding with a picket fence.

In two series overseas Snow had taken 58 wickets in 390 overs. In the process he became the world's most feared and admired fast bowler.

This pulsating head of steam could never last, and indeed it didn't. Mentally and probably physically exhausted by these exertions, Snow found it hard to return home to the relatively humdrum world of county cricket in which he was expected to perform. He couldn't cope with it and was unable, except on rare occasions, to raise his game. For him the county circuit, albeit that it had got him where he was in the first place, was incompatible with Test cricket and its demands.

Nobody quite seemed to understand. In 1971 Snow was somewhat publicly dropped from the Sussex team for not trying, an accusation he found hard to deny. As I said earlier, Snow was a thoroughbred more akin to a Nijinsky or Shergar than a Red Rum, the king of stayers. He needed to be saved up for the big occasions and not asked, as it were, to run in a selling hurdle at Plumpton.

Not that Snow was an easy chap. He wasn't. He could be a cold fish, shy, solitary and often ill at ease in public. Moody and awkward he sometimes was. Very fit and lean too – no smoking or drinking – a fine physical specimen whose mystique made him very attractive to women. Jenny, his wife, discovered him, I think, when she was working for Benson and Hedges who sponsored one of the county one-day competitions. Inseparable since then, which must have been the early seventies, they have two daughters, Katherine and Suzanne, and dogs. Always dogs. Enormous German Shepherds would invade the dressing room from time to time. They had lots of them. Snow loves his dogs and indeed, like many owners, takes on something of a likeness to them. Donkeys he loves too and possibly pigs as well, although of that I'm not sure. But I think I can safely say that Snow gets on better with animals than humans. He is not the only one.

It was in the early seventies as I was just embarking upon my career that I first really encountered Snow. We travelled together in his bright orange BMW to play in a match against Somerset at Taunton. I don't think we talked very much, and he drove rather fast. I suppose fast bowlers do that sort of thing. But it was during that trip that we began to forge the beginnings of a friendship. The reason for this wasn't initially obvious, but what I think Snow liked about me was my style of batting. You see, I was a blocker who tried very hard above all else not to get out. It was hard work, of course, and not easy. At Taunton in Sussex's first innings I batted for 4½ hours for 52 runs. It was very dull for the crowd and everyone else, but Snow loved it and appreciated its value. What it did for him was to keep him resting happily in the pavilion for longer than he otherwise might. He liked that enormously. It didn't always work out like that, but Snow had spotted my potential and how it could well serve his cause. By and large we've remained friends ever since.

While Snow did not try very hard in my early days at Sussex, he was amused by the youngsters who seemed to pose less threat to him in the authority stakes. Mark Faber made him laugh, a young player of outstanding natural talent whom Snow nicknamed 'Racer' after his Porsche which sped him to matches up and down the country. Faber was never going to be in the game for the long haul and so played more or less as an amateur and got away with most things. Whilst this irritated Tony Greig, I think Snow was rather jealous. It was in a way how he would like to have played the game himself.

Faber, Barclay and a young lad called Jeremy Groome constantly teased Snow and, bearing in mind his status in the game, were most disrespectful. "Going to bowl fast enough to knock the bails off today, Snowy?" was the sort of banter that drifted about the dressing room. Strangely enough Snow rather enjoyed it all, and so did we.

At Old Trafford in 1974 Lancashire batted first in a championship match played on a green pitch. Before we took the field Snow pronounced that "All captains should be banned", an assertion based I think on the fact that ours, Tony Buss on this occasion, had lost the toss. Tactics didn't come into it. Snow bowled poorly and without spark in helpful conditions, but he did persuade Barry Wood, the Lancashire opening batsman, quite early on to pull a long hop into the hands of square leg. As Frank Hayes came onto the field to replace Wood, Snow put his arms in the air and shouted out as if in encouragement, "Come on, spread out, chaps, and let's see if we can trap another one." We didn't and, on a day made for seam bowlers, two Sussex spinners, Barclay and Waller, bowled the lion's share of the overs. And here we were, playing with one of the great post-war fast bowlers, possibly the best since Trueman and Statham had ruled supreme.

By 1976, in looking for new ways in which to motivate Snow, Greig decided to promote him to open the batting in the John Player Sunday League. Snow was amused by the idea and took his new position much more seriously than he did his bowling. It was a fresh challenge. Snow became the first of the pinch hitters, long before the term had been invented. As a result we came perilously close to winning the competition and only stumbled in the final match against Warwickshire at Edgbaston. Still, runners-up was a fair reward for this unlikely initiative.

I think there is little doubt that Snow used to get bored and particularly so with cricket. Day in, day out, there just wasn't enough in it to keep him interested. He was an unusual chap, a deep thinker at times but not so good at expressing himself verbally. Captaincy might have lit the touch paper, but I never remember him having a go at that. I wonder whether he would have taken it seriously. Possibly.

There was an occasion when he was playing for Sussex against Leicestershire at Leicester (I wasn't actually there) when he was required to bowl all morning in the drizzle with a wet ball. Fed up with this impairment, he exchanged the ball after lunch for a bar of red soap which he had fetched from the shower. First ball after the interval he bowled it at Peter Marner, the Leicestershire middle order batsman, who struck it boldly. The ball disintegrated into thousands of pieces. The Sussex scorer made a mark in the scorebook with an asterisk and an arrow under which he simply wrote 'ball exploded'.

In 1976 Snow, aged 35, was in the twilight of his career and, although blest with enormous talent, he would never have made much money from the game. He wrote a slightly disgruntled book called *Cricket Rebel* and two books of poems, none of which could be described as best-sellers. Then his immediate prospects were saved in 1977 by the advent of Kerry Packer's World Series Cricket. Packer was prepared to pay what was a lot of money in those days to persuade players to join in with plans which defied the established world of cricket. Snow, with his captain Tony Greig, was personally implicated in the court case and attended the hearings wearing a suit and tie – he didn't often do that – looking very much the City gentleman. There was never much doubt about the outcome – Restraint of Trade being the issue in question – and Snow was able to retire to a country house in Sussex which out of deep gratitude he called 'Packway'.

Now in his seventieth year I suppose you could say that Snow is more or less retired. He walks the dogs, sorts out the donkeys and plays a bit of golf. Unsurprisingly he is a fair player although, when I played with him recently, he confessed to having a bit of an off day. We all know about them. For all that, he showed patience in adversity and restraint in his language when he topped his drive or heaved the ball out of the bounds. It was a beautiful spring day, blossom on the trees and bluebells in the woods too. Plenty of opportunity to look at those. What was interesting and amusing was that Snow worried more than I would have expected about his own golf – stance, hands, head, shoulders – just as I did about my batting all those years back. "Just watch the ball and hit it," Snow would say to me in desperation from the other side of the dressing room. Now I could have said the same to him as he over-attentively struck putts with neither correct pace nor direction. Tea and cake were placed on the table afterwards outside the clubhouse, a civilised world and a far cry from the menace of international cricket.

I think that's enough of Snow. An extraordinary man with a lot of edge, but all the same someone for whom I have a great liking. It would be dull if we were all the same, and Snow certainly isn't. He will undoubtedly go down as one of England's great fast bowlers.

Ian Terence Botham

Born: Heswall, Cheshire, 24 November 1955

102 Tests for England (1977-1992)
5,200 runs at an average of 33.54, 14 centuries
383 wickets at an average of 28.40
120 catches

402 first-class matches (1974-1993)
19,399 runs at an average of 33.97, 38 centuries
1,172 wickets at an average of 27.22

Ian Botham was the man who, in the early 1980s, did more than anybody to create a resurgence of interest in cricket in England. In almost everything he did on the field, and indeed off it, he captured the popular imagination.

After a spell at Lord's, where his bowling in the nets was considered a joke, he returned home to Somerset where he rapidly turned into England's leading all-rounder, filling the place in the England team vacated by Tony Greig's departure to World Series Cricket. In his first seven Tests he hit three hundreds and five times took five wickets in an innings. His century and 13 wickets against India in Bombay in February 1980 is arguably the greatest all-round match performance in the history of Test cricket.

Appointed England captain in succession to Mike Brearley, he had the misfortune to start with two series against the West Indies but, relieved of the captaincy in 1981, he enjoyed his finest hour: winning three successive Ashes Tests with breathtaking performances with bat and ball.

Controversy dogged his later career, but again he inspired the nation with a series of gruelling charity walks on behalf of child leukaemia research.

Ian Botham

So far in these sketches I have referred to my subjects either by their Christian or surname. I simply haven't got the heart to do that in this case. For me Botham has never been Ian nor Beefy but just simply 'Both', an unimaginative and unexotic abbreviation for one so well known but one with which I feel comfortable and I'm sure he does too. It will have to do.

I first bumped into 'Both' at Lord's in August 1973. Sussex had been playing Middlesex in the semi-finals of the Gillette Cup and, although I wasn't playing, I was twelfth or thirteenth man and was there in the dressing room. Amidst much tension, Sussex won the game by five runs. After all the excitement had died down and the dust was beginning to settle upon one of Sussex's more glorious days, I was returning to my car parked at the Nursery end, a second-hand Austin 1100 (cream coloured) of which I was justifiably very proud, having only recently passed my driving test.

I was approached somewhat out of the blue by a tallish, slim lad. "Any chance of giving me a lift to Brighton?" he said "I'm playing tomorrow in my first match for Somerset in the Sunday league. If you're going that way I'd be very grateful." I think I knew who he was as we had already played against each other earlier in the season, Sussex 2nd XI v. MCC Young Cricketers.

"I'd love to," I replied, "but sadly I'm staying up in London tonight to see friends and not travelling down to Hove until tomorrow." "Oh, pity," he said and strolled off into the late evening sunshine, presumably to catch a train. Ever since I've felt this was something of a missed opportunity. I could have gone down in history as the man who drove him to his first match.

'Both' was lucky to spend a couple of years on the ground staff at Lord's under the watchful and probably anxious eyes of coaches Len Muncer and Harry Sharp. I daresay these were wild days for 'Both' but, in amongst his high spirits, he was grounded with a sound batting and bowling technique. As a batsman he played very straight and showed the full face of the bat to the ball whilst, with the ball, a classical sideways action emerged and was later pulled into shape by his mentor at Somerset, Tom Cartwright. As Geoffrey Boycott would say, "the lad had good technique." This was, of course, accompanied by a lively and laddish spirit. Whether he was having a good or bad day, Both was always jolly, full of beans, up for a beer (sometimes several) and endearingly generous. He never let failure put him off and took success in his stride as well. His goodwill was both unsophisticated and genuine. He was never dull.

I think it was this extraordinary spirit that emerged so dramatically at Headingley in 1981. If you remember, the game was up; England had all but lost the match when Dilley joined Both for a final fling. And that's just what it was: a relaxed, controlled slog with nothing more to lose. Few would have had the nerve to play as he did. Australia were caught in the storm and powerless to reverse the tidal wave of Botham. A glorious fluke, village-green almost, and it came off. It was Both's day; he made it his day.

I suppose you might say that Both was erratic, but there was a certain consistency in his erratic nature. His wildness was quite predictable.

He loves fishing and so do I. Despite his gregarious nature he loves nothing more than to be wading, deep and dangerously up to his chest, in the current. Not a natural loner he does, though, love to immerse himself in nature but with friends near at hand with whom to share a good lunch. In 1996 we were in New Zealand for England's tour there and, on a day off, Both organised a salmon-fishing trip for the keen fishermen in the party. Not just any old run-of-the-mill trip but one which involved jet boats which would speed us up river to our starting point.

Things didn't go to plan. Heavy rains in the mountains had rendered the river unnavigable. Play had to be abandoned. Instead, Both persuaded our guides to take us all out to lunch high up in the hills where we came upon a large log cabin, roaring fire and a lot of wine. Rarely have I seen so much food and drink consumed.

I saw first-hand the tentacles of danger that surround Both on a day off. He seemed to drink a remarkable quantity of liquor without appearing to be in the least bit drunk, which is more than could be said about one or two others in the party. On the way home our very sporting guides tentatively invited us to join a drinks party with their friends down on the low-lying land upon which the sun was now shining. As we approached the party, we could see the gathering of guests, all with drinks in their hands. 'Both' took one look at them and at the marquee on the lawn and, much to my relief, shouted, "Drive on, driver, I don't think we shall be staying here." In twenty seconds we drove in and out of their party, leaving the guests standing about, looking startled.

He was a wild man, fallible of course, brilliant at times, competitive when the mood took him and very jovial; strangely with no real ego. To me he was just 'Both'.

He has always reminded me of a rainbow trout. They are natives of America, introduced to this country in the 19th century. They, like Both, are wild and aggressive creatures which dash about enthusiastically without much thought for the consequences. If something tasty floats past their noses, they are likely to rush at it – impulsive and instinctive. This makes Both a very catchable fish, a big one too and not too familiar with cunning and guile. Once on the hook, the two are great fighters, terrific sport pound for pound and prepared for a long struggle. They are fit specimens and will glisten and shimmer when landed on the bank, so good in fact that they have to be put back to fight another day. Neither would recognise danger if it ambushed them.

Both is a doer, a physical man; he likes to be at the forefront of the action. His charity work for Leukaemia Research has been outstanding and never more so than when he walked with friends to raise funds. By contrast, he seems somewhat less well suited to broadcasting. The poor man is stuck in a box where he tries to be thoughtful and measured, but the gift of the gab is not really his thing. Neither was leadership. He had far too much to offer to be wrapped up with the cares of the world. Players of rare talent are so important to any team and often too vulnerable or naïve when elevated to positions in which they then struggle to cope. We all saw Both disintegrate before our eyes when his reign as captain of England came to an end at Lord's with a pair of noughts against Australia. His pride was surely dented, but deep down it may have come as a merciful release. The consequences were profound.

One of the most revered, respected and much talked about characters in the game was Both's first captain of Somerset, Brian Close, described by the great *Times* writer Alan Gibson as 'the bald-headed blighter'. It would appear that Close, a prodigious young talent in his day, had the measure of Botham. He chain-smoked his way through each day, conducting affairs by leading from the front on the field and positioning himself unhelmeted and perilously close to each batsman at short-leg. Off the field, before and after his innings, he would be constantly on the telephone to his bookie to whom he imparted most of his cash. He was an inveterate gambler and, in his own way, lived his life on the edge. At Hove in 1976, early days for Both and me, I was given an unexpectedly long bowling spell by my captain, Tony Greig, in the course of which I bamboozled Close with a ball of unexpected cunning. It was one of those balls which slipped out from time to time, the sort that, once released, caused me to rush down the pitch and try to capture it before the batsman could whack it. This was a particularly bad one, and indeed I may even have let out a little shout upon releasing it. It bounced once and, dam busters style, was just about to bounce again when Close let fly at it with his Stuart Surridge bat. But, instead of stroking the ball majestically to the boundary, he merely hacked it off the inside edge back onto his stumps. Close, bowled Barclay 59. An ignominious dismissal and all watched by the pup Botham from the other end. Both made his first major impact with the bat in this match and was dismissed just three short of what would have been his maiden first-class century. At lunchtime Close made as if to try and strangle me; I felt quite the old pro.

Just two years later Both and I were locked in serious combat in the Gillette Cup final at Lord's. A full house it was, a sunny day and Somerset clear favourites with their star players, Viv Richards and Joel Garner, at their best. It did not take long for Somerset to reach 30, mainly due to some wayward radar from Imran who bowled with great pace but faulty direction. Nerves and over-excitement can affect even the most seasoned campaigners. Wides are unwelcome wherever you're playing, but at Lord's they had a withering effect upon our early morale.

By the time Both joined Richards, we had clambered back into the game and I was brought on to bowl against two of the world's hardest hitters and most imposing batsmen. To my immense relief they were in consolidating, rather than biffing, mood and I was allowed to settle. Although Both did on one occasion come down the pitch and drive me imperiously through the covers for four runs – Bishen Bedi used to applaud batsmen on such occasions but I thought better of it – Viv and Both were inclined to bide their time before unleashing any out-and-out assault. I got away with it, and Both proceeded to play what I would call a very polite and responsible innings of 80 while wickets fell the other end. The result was a less than dramatic 207 for Somerset in their 60 overs, a very gettable target even by Sussex's erratic standards.

Botham and Garner bowled in harness, with the crowd warming to the occasion and by now well fortified by alcoholic lunches. It was a hostile affair. Gehan Mendis and I were greeted by a series of balls banged hard into the pitch with mean and malicious intent. For some unknown reason I couldn't resist Both's bowling. Normally the most obdurate of blockers, the blood fairly coursed through my veins when I saw him approaching the crease. Sportingly he would show you his bouncer; he whacked it into the turf and, for once, I didn't disappoint in reply. I had a go – the cut or pull – it was a strange and unlikely rivalry. He would do the same when I, with rather more half volleys, bowled at him. The more I scattered men to the boundary, the more he tried to clear them. Neither of us normally lasted long.

Returning to bowl as he did immediately after the tea interval, he started unsurprisingly with a bouncer – a long-hop really, if I'm honest. I shaped to pull the ball with vigour through mid-wicket but caught it depressingly high on the bat and sent up a skier wide of mid-on. At first I didn't think Roebuck was going to make it. I shouted loudly for a run, hoping to put him off, but sadly that didn't fool him and he completed the catch. Once again I had succumbed to a bad ball from Both, and I slumped off disconsolately having lost the battle. Amidst all this and despite my being considered something of a toff and Both a wild creature, we got on rather well together. We held each other in an unlikely degree of respect.

Time went by and Both became very famous, but he always combined his talent with the lumbering gait of a farm labourer. He never forgot his roots nor did he forget his friends. I rarely remember him suffering an injury; by and large he came from tough and strong stock – or so I thought.

One year, in my early days of captaincy, Sussex played Somerset at Taunton in April, the first championship match of the season. The Somerset players in the field were well wrapped up in thermals and all, while Mendis and I had the luxury of gloves to keep our hands warm while we batted. In the chilly West Country air I spent much of the morning fending off the threat of Colin Dredge's medium pace while I selflessly left Mendis to deal with Garner at the other end. Midway through the morning's play Dredge, in a bid to get the score moving, bowled me a long-hop outside my off stump. With all my might and energy I aimed a vicious square cut at it. I misjudged the bounce and, instead of smiting the ball fiercely past cover point, merely top-edged it quite slowly and with some loop at catchable height towards second slip.

There Both, unfortunately for him, was not alert to the opportunity of catching me out. My batting had, in fact, lulled him into deep slumber and he stood motionless, his hands upon his knees, as the ball travelled towards him. He never did move until the ball struck him firmly in those parts where manhood could be placed in severe peril by such a sudden direct blow. Clutching the tender spot, the great man let out a huge roar of pain and anguish that caused the few spectators that there were to look up briefly from their newspapers, whereupon he collapsed with a dull thud to the ground, moaning forlornly.

It proved hard to console a man struck down on a cold day by an attempted square cut but his sizeable body had, all the same, to be removed from the field. This was no easy task, no stretchers in evidence, so he was unceremoniously carried off by three Somerset and two Sussex players (Le Roux and Phillipson) who emerged from the pavilion to lend a hand. Meanwhile I, as captain and opening batsman, lived on to fight another day and earned more than my fair share of admiration from a Sussex team who were very grateful that, with one telling blow, I had laid waste England's number one all-rounder.

It can't always have been easy for Both with his special talent for cricket, admired for great and heroic feats with bat and ball. After all he is an ordinary chap, a friendly fellow with no great complicated powers of thought or intellect. And yet he found himself surrounded by academics: Roebuck, Marks and Popplewell at Somerset and Brearley, his mentor and leader in his heyday with England. His greatest strength was that, despite occasional binges of excess, he rubbed along with everyone.

I couldn't help but like the man; I always feel an empathy for anyone who loves fishing. Right from the beginning he was just 'Both' to me. I don't feel he's really changed that much over the years.

John Woodcock

Jim Swanton

Christopher Martin-Jenkins

Robin Marlar

Four writers

John Charles Woodcock

Born: Longparish, Hampshire, 7 August 1926

Cricket Correspondent, The Times, *1954-1988*
Editor, Wisden Cricketers' Almanack, *1981-1986*

Ernest William Swanton

Born: Forest Hill, London, 11 February 1907
Died: Canterbury, Kent, 22 January 2000

3 first-class matches (1937-1938)

Cricket Correspondent, London Evening Standard, *1927-1939*
Cricket Correspondent, Daily Telegraph, *1946-1975*
Editorial Director, The Cricketer, *1967-1988*

Christopher Dennis Alexander Martin-Jenkins

Born: Peterborough, 20 January 1945
Died: Rudgwick, Sussex, 1 January 2013

Cricket Correspondent, BBC, *1973-1980, 1985-1991*
Editorial Director, The Cricketer, *1981-1991*
Cricket Correspondent, Daily Telegraph, *1990-1999*
Cricket Correspondent, The Times, *1999-2008*

Robin Geoffrey Marlar

Born: Eastbourne, Sussex, 2 January 1931

289 first-class matches (1951-1968)

970 wickets at an average of 25.22

Cricket Correspondent, Sunday Times, *1970-1996*

Four writers

Down the years few sports have inspired such a rich variety of prose as cricket. The pen and indeed the voice, too, have influenced many thousands of cricket lovers by way of newspapers, magazines, books and, of course, the spoken word. Such are the interest and absorption that Radio 4 still devotes, in its *Test Match Special* programme, a full day to commentary and discussion. Hour upon hour dedicated, ball by ball, to cricket. I suppose it is the nature of the game that lends itself to such obsessive attention. Cricket, even in its more exciting moments, prompts reflection as the plot slowly unfolds. There is time for the writers to ponder and so perhaps relate more closely to all those sharing their day.

I have chosen here just four of my favourite writers: Jim Swanton, John Woodcock, Robin Marlar and Christopher Martin-Jenkins. There are plenty of others of course: John Arlott, Brian Johnston, Neville Cardus and Alan Gibson to name a few, but I know them less well. Cardus, I never had the chance to meet. All these writers have used their words with skill and, whilst they have basked in a world of unusual characters some of whom they may even have hero-worshipped somewhat, they have pursued their powers of description to shed a rich glow upon the game and its followers.

These great writers – journalists somehow seems the wrong word for them – were rarely to be seen sheltering in press boxes. They preferred to potter around the ground, meet up with friends and generally capture the atmosphere of the occasion. Swanton might be found in the Committee Room or, better still, the President's Box. The others, sometimes needing a telephone from which to file their copy, might dive bravely into the press box or tent towards the end of the day.

I remember first meeting John Woodcock at Ilkeston in Derbyshire in April. It was Sussex's first match of the season in 1976 and freezing cold it was, too. Despite a slow pitch and helpful bowling conditions I had batted far longer than usual but, once dismissed, took myself for a walk around the ground with a fellow sufferer, Mark Faber. We found Woodcock sitting, well wrapped up in a coat and scarf, on the far side of the field, watching the cricket with his dog and enjoying one of the game's less visited first-class venues. He was one of the several spectators enduring a match in which the run rate rarely crept above two an over. Plenty of time for reflection.

The Sussex run rate would have finished well below two an over if it had not been for the strange disease, known as the yips, which afflicted poor Fred Swarbrook of Derbyshire during the match. The unlucky man became paralysed with fear when he bowled his slow left-armers, and his fingers rendered him unable to release the ball with any certainty as to its subsequent whereabouts. I faced his first ball of the match which shot over my head and the wicket-keeper Bob Taylor's too, and sped off for four runs. The next one bounced twice, and I chopped it away for three behind square on the off-side and was much relieved to get down the other end. It was horrible to watch a fellow player suffer so dreadfully. Just eight months earlier at Hove, Swarbrook had taken nine for 20 against Sussex on a wet pitch, the best bowling figures of that season. Despite many efforts and much psychological help Swarbrook never fully recovered and he disappeared from the game only to be rediscovered by me in Kimberley, South Africa, when I was playing for the Orange Free State. I encountered him in the Griqualand side as a staunch middle-order batsman, his bowling just a vexed memory from a past life.

For Woodcock this must have been just another county match and possibly a bit of a sweat to drive all the way up the M1 to Ilkeston from Longparish in Hampshire. Yet his enthusiasm for the game, a stodgy one in this case, was captivating, and we chatted for some time by his car before moving on. Woodcock's colleagues would have been huddled up in the press tent with all the facts and figures at their finger-tips but possibly less in tune with the atmosphere and ambience of the Rutland ground at Ilkeston.

Woodcock's verdict on my own laboured effort with the bat managed to be both truthful and kind, which cannot have been entirely easy in the circumstances:

> Barclay was first in and eighth out, a resistance based on forward defence and infinite watchfulness. His dedication to the game is a byword in Sussex. He is said to start preparing for his innings at crack of dawn.

One day, in rather the same way as Glenn Turner of Worcestershire has (Turner was almost exclusively defensive at one time), Barclay could develop into a consistent scorer. By the time he was yorked yesterday he had been in for 65 overs, a horribly long while for 41 runs but useful experience and a valuable innings all the same.

Long before my time I believe there would have been a much warmer, closer relationship between the press and players. Life on tours, for example, was taken at a slower pace – more time to breathe and reflect. The game in many ways was less fraught and journalists would turn a blind eye to much that went on and were less likely to betray any confidences. There would have been something of an unwritten code of behaviour.

Much of the trust of this earlier era has been eroded as newspaper circulation has become more competitive and journalists have had to battle to find space for their stories. Good writing has gradually given way to news stories with players caught in the middle of it all, not quite knowing where they stood. So journalism has become more of a mad scramble with many of the old values blown away. In South Africa in 1995 Ray Illingworth, the England manager, treated the press as he had done twenty-five years earlier when he himself was captain, with plenty of words spoken off the cuff, tongue in cheek mostly and without much thought for the consequences. He found himself frequently tripped up, compromised and damaged. The press game had changed its rules, and mercy was in short supply.

I imagine that in the old days it was easier for the press and players to become friends. There would have been a more relaxed atmosphere about first-class matches, many of which were played amidst the informality of towns like Eastbourne, Bath, Cheltenham or Buxton. There, the likes of Swanton, Woodcock, Marlar, Martin-Jenkins and others would be seen wandering about, meeting friends and chatting to players who might be strolling around the ground in search of an ice-cream by way of consolation for failure on the field. Life was more easy-going then; cricketers were able to breathe more freely and share in this pleasure.

To some extent players will feed off the press who in turn will see those same players as a source of privileged information. Cricketers like to see their names in the papers and are indeed flattered by the attention they receive from an association with journalists. I remember being quite excited when Matthew Engel asked me in South Africa to do a piece with him for, I think, the *Guardian*. At the time I was assistant manager to Ray Illingworth and felt proud and uplifted to catch the eye of Engel. The England players were much the same as me. Journalists would befriend them, buy them drinks, take them out to dinner, chat them up, if you like, and get them on their side as a trusted friend. But the competitive nature of sports editors back at home has little time for humour and conviviality and knows no bounds. The journalists on tour and scattered around cricket grounds are mere agents in the field and, if they want to keep their jobs, have to be sharp, on the ball and opportunistic. Players, whilst enjoying themselves and playing their cricket, must be watchful and on their guard. I remember quite vividly in Zimbabwe in 1996, when I was manager of an England team that was making a fair hash of its campaign, Charles Colville from Sky television approached me with words that sent a slight chill down my spine. "Johnny," he said, "the press are on the rampage." With the bit between their teeth, so-called friends can turn into pack animals hungry for the kill. It happens time and time again. All is well until things go wrong.

Whilst Woodcock, Swanton and Marlar formed the old guard, Martin-Jenkins from a younger generation wrote with that same fluency, balance, perception and, above all, good judgement. Marlar could be fierce, of course, a natural bruiser who loves nothing more than a bit of combat and confrontation. When he sensed a hint of weakness, he went for the jugular. I experienced this at first hand when he led the revolt which overthrew the Sussex committee in 1997. His rhetoric was powerful; he had done his homework well. I was struck dumb for once in my life and cowered low in my chair at the Annual General Meeting, allowing the storm to sweep over before slipping quietly away into the night. Marlar could be quite frightening and yet, beneath his cantankerous spirit, there was a deep warmth and love for cricket. This I much respected. I think, more than any other writer I have known, Marlar really got to grips with things and thrashed them about. His pieces in the *Sunday Times* would be written to stir up the senses and were certainly never dull.

Back in 1977, when I was a real youngster and just pressing my claims for a first-team place with Sussex, the world of cricket became absorbed by the challenge to the game of Kerry Packer's World Series proposals. All this came rather out of the blue to me. Tony Greig, my Sussex captain for whom the players had great admiration, was Packer's right-hand man and had helped recruit players to his cause, lured by impressive sums of money. Marlar was not one to stand idly by and shelter from this storm. No, not him. He waded out into the deep and got stuck in. The row, if I remember rightly, peaked in a television studio with Packer and Marlar seated either side of David Frost who acted as referee. While Marlar was largely outmanoeuvred by the slick and brutish Packer, he put up a vehement defence for the soul and history of the game. As Marlar battled valiantly on against a cold but supremely professional adversary, the warmth of his commitment to cricket shone through.

Whether fighting a lost cause or not, Marlar was always true to himself and consistent in his battles which were not infrequent. On one occasion quite recently, when he was President of MCC, he attended an Oxford University match in the Parks. Aggrieved by the shouting and general noise on the field, he strode majestically out to the pitch and up to the players themselves, demanding that they showed the game greater respect and cut out the row. The participants must have been quite startled and possibly amused, but I dare say Marlar's stand had the desired effect. He would have been a very good man to have at one's side in the trenches.

By contrast, the sense of gravitas which Swanton exuded, his self-importance and air of grandeur, trumped the expertise of his contemporaries, and his presence on any ground, for the most part in the home counties and south-east, somehow altered the chemistry of the day. His influence was very considerable, and he knew it. The selectors and members of MCC and its committees read his articles in the *Telegraph* and took much of them to heart. A good write-up from Swanton was worth its weight in gold and players stood to attention, as it were, and looked sharp if ever he was spotted on the ground. In a funny sort of way he was quite powerful and someone to keep on your side, if possible. He would have made an impressive MCC President or perhaps even Archbishop of Canterbury – conceivably both.

I think it is no secret that Swanton loved the rich and grand and rarely missed the chance to chat to a duke or duchess, should they happen to be close at hand. Perhaps it was therefore no real surprise that our first encounter took place at the Eton and Harrow match which in 1970 was played on the sixth form ground at Harrow instead of Lord's which was still recovering from the effect of South Africa's aborted tour that same summer. Swanton was very much in his element at Harrow and we, as young players, were flattered and pleased to see him. It was a chance to make a name for ourselves in the *Telegraph*. Although we won the match, I somewhat blotted my own copy-book by having a huge slog to leg, head in the air, from a gentle in-swinger and lost my leg stump. Swanton had spotted a large gasometer not far distant on which was written in large white letters NO as a directive to aircraft landing at Northolt. He firmly suggested in his article that I should take heed of this message.

Despite his penchant for grandeur, much of it tongue in cheek and rather expected of him, Swanton could also be kind and supportive, albeit with a distinct leaning towards public schools and Oxbridge. He invited me to join his own cricket club, the Arabs, and immediately selected me to tour Barbados early in 1974. It was a baptism of fire in which we were blasted around the island by bat and ball. Even the hotel waiters, recruited as net bowlers, inflicted pain upon the precious Arab fingers. Collis King, of West Indian international fame, hit the ball back past me so fiercely when I bowled that it ricocheted off the concrete white wall of the sight screen and returned conveniently to my feet, ready for me to bowl again. We did a lot of losing, and Swanton was somewhat puzzled by our lack of success despite the joy of being in Barbados and the delights it had to offer apart from cricket.

Without doubt Swanton enriched the game, added colour to any occasion; pontificated and laid down the law but also saw the funny side of things, especially in later years when his views had perhaps softened a touch. He loved an audience, a great broadcaster in every sense with end-of-day Test match summaries on BBC television that have never been surpassed.

Just as I am sure that many writers admire their favourite cricketers (Swanton certainly thought the world of Tony Greig for a while), so cricketers in turn respect the talents and authority of many writers. Good writers somehow make it look easy. A quick single to get off the mark; they find their rhythm and it flows. And I imagine that there's not much time at the end of each day to redraft and alter the shape of a piece, let alone correct the grammar. I wonder sometimes if it is actually rather easier for a batsman to build an innings for his side, even if the ending is often both abrupt and unexpected.

I come to the fourth of my great writers and commentators, Christopher Martin-Jenkins. He was the consummate all-rounder, as much at home with the pen as in the commentary box, on the cricket field or the golf course. He probably worked harder than anyone I have known, writing and speaking as many words about the game as anyone has ever done. For years he was the BBC's cricket correspondent before Jonathan Agnew took over, and he also found time to edit the *Cricketer International* magazine. The *Times* and *Telegraph* readers enjoyed the balanced Martin-Jenkins take on cricket matches for goodness knows how long. He could be tough, determined and unafraid to speak his mind courageously on thorny issues. But what I found forever surprising about him was his ability to turn from the straight man of measured and calm judgement to an after-dinner speaker where he combined mimicry, anecdote and punch-line jokes. As an entertainer, be it at a cricket do or whatever, he was hard to surpass.

Without doubt Martin-Jenkins became the voice of cricket; he spoke with authority, yet never laid down the law. He had firm beliefs on what is right and wrong but didn't go on about things. Martin-Jenkins would surely have made an excellent headmaster had he been attracted, as indeed his son Robin has, to the teaching profession. Beneath a facade of gentleness lay a competitive streak which I found was most evident on the golf course. He liked to play well (don't we all?) and indeed preferred to win, but his mishits were rarely encapsulated by anything stronger than a fiercely muttered 'fiddle-de-dee'. That was about as bad as it ever got.

I think I shall end this piece by returning as a sort of postscript to John Woodcock, for me the JS Bach of cricket prose, for whom rich melodies abound and where counterpoint enhances the harmonies. For me Woodcock reigns supreme; he combines humility with authority. He told me firmly that I should stamp my mark on the tour of Zimbabwe as manager in 1996. I failed him in that. Afterwards, Swanton had stern words with me too about my handling of certain issues. But, above all else, they both cared and took trouble, and that counts for a lot in friendship.

Woodcock loves to see his friends fishing on his beloved River Avon at Upper Woodford in Wiltshire. For several years Mike Atherton and I have benefited from his generosity and, although I have never actually seen Woodcock fish, I suspect he would cast a fly with the same fluency as he writes. To see him standing on the river bank watching the water is as much a comfort as it is to see him at a cricket ground watching cricket.

Let it be hoped that, as the game advances into the 21st century and different pressures emerge to upset its balance, the relationship between cricket and its great writers can strengthen rather than diminish the stature of the game.

Malcolm Denzil Marshall

Born: Bridgetown, Barbados, 18 April 1958
Died: Bridgetown, Barbados, 4 November 1999

81 Tests for West Indies (1978-1991)

1,810 runs at an average of 18.85
376 wickets at an average of 20.94

408 first-class matches (1978-1996)

11,004 runs at an average of 24.83, 7 centuries
1,651 wickets at an average of 19.10

Malcolm Marshall was a right-arm fast bowler, for a time in the early 1980s the fastest in the world. His career coincided with a great era of West Indian quick bowlers – Roberts, Holding, Garner, Walsh and Ambrose among them – and his final Test bowling average was the best of them all. He was also, by some margin, the best batsmen among them, scoring 10 fifties in Tests.

He was not a tall man, but he trained hard, he was a thinking bowler and on the county circuit, playing for Hampshire from 1979 to 1993, his stamina was prodigious. In one summer, 1982, he bowled more than 1,000 overs in first-class and limited-over cricket, his total of 160 wickets in all matches the highest in a season since 1967. He also scored valuable runs – 891 in all cricket that summer and 1,372 in 1990.

His most astonishing performance was in the Headingley Test of 1984 when his left thumb was doubly fractured while fielding on the first morning. Against advice he went out to bat one-handed, to enable his team-mate Larry Gomes to reach his century, then – with his injury encased in plaster – he took seven wickets for 53 runs in the England second innings.

Malcolm Marshall

This is quite a story, an unusual one of which I am not in the least bit proud.

I tapped at the crease with my bat while Marshall reached the end of his run-up. Normally I didn't mind facing fast bowlers, even the fiercer ones. If nothing else, death came quickly and often without fuss. Nothing like the tortuous agony of being tormented by spin. Yes, it demanded courage and a little technique but not so much brain and was less humiliating.

"Who's the fastest bowler you've ever faced?" I am always being asked that. Roberts perhaps, Holding, Daniel, Hadlee or Procter on his day. Walsh was pretty quick too, and Croft, and Sylvester Clarke whom I nearly forgot. He could be lethal. Imran Khan as well, but I only ever faced him in the nets and I don't think that really counts. All of them were fast on their day but none more likely to get you out than Marshall. He was the best, I should say, and probably the most dangerous too.

Marshall approached the crease from a wide arc with short rhythmical strides. He was not tall for a fast bowler, probably less than six foot, and built more for stamina than pace. He was a thoroughbred – stocky, strong and athletic – more of a Derby runner than an out-and-out sprinter. He was certainly a stayer and a willing one at that.

It was August, cricket week at Eastbourne, the first day of the match against Hampshire, and we were in trouble. For various reasons we were missing Parker, Greig, Gould and Le Roux. Imran was back from the World Cup but with sore shins and so only able to bat, not bowl, while I was handicapped by a damaged finger which impeded my freedom with bat and ball. In short, Sussex were in a sorry state and not best equipped to face the most incisive and penetrating bowler in the world.

Marshall had savaged our early batting. Mendis, Cowan, Green, Heath, Colin and Alan Wells had all fallen cheaply. The score was 83 for six when I joined Imran who remained our main hope of salvaging respectability and avoiding humiliation.

You will notice the name Cowan in our line-up. Not a household name in the world of cricket, he was playing on the back of a stunning performance in a World Cup warm-up match against Australia earlier in the summer. In it he bowled 8.5 overs and took five for 17, a performance which earned him the nickname of 'Wrecker Ralph', that being his Christian name. It is not plain how this achievement bounced him up to number three in the batting order, but in the event he was out first ball and I don't recall his bowling. For what it's worth and irrelevant too in this context, Ralph played football with some success for Lewes Town and now teaches geography at Caterham School in Surrey. He was briefly one of my favourite cricketers but, to be fair, one who rarely assisted the Sussex cause. In that he was not alone.

By early afternoon Imran and I had staged something of a recovery, taking the score to 145 for six. I had only scored 13, but Imran had just reached his hundred. It was a warm day at Eastbourne, a holiday crowd and atmosphere to match. Picnic lunches, a beer or two, a bottle of wine, strawberries and raspberries were the order of the day – short sleeves, shorts and sunbathing too for the more exotic.

I loved Eastbourne and loved playing there. In the old days it was one of the best batting pitches in the country, evenly grassed and low of bounce. The ball came on nicely into the middle of the bat. I had even made some runs at Eastbourne from time to time, never a hundred but 60s, 70s and 80s, though the plurals attached to those figures may be a little fanciful. In 1977, I think it was, I got struck on the ear by a ball from Collis King when going well and had to spend an afternoon in Eastbourne's hospital, but mainly I have happy memories of this famous seaside town. There was tennis just across the road at Devonshire Park where I watched my daughter play in the finals of the under-12 Sussex Tennis Tournament on Centre Court. She hit an easy forehand into the net when on match point and two games later lost the match. Ice creams all round to counter the bitter taste of disappointment. The courts are but a stone's throw from the sea, pebbly beach, promenade and pier, where the band plays and soothes away the anxieties of everyday life.

With the sea air carrying with it the smell of seaweed and salt, I was now aware that Marshall, with his curved run-up, not dissimilar to that of John Price of Middlesex in his heyday, was preparing to bowl. He ran in on tip toes. "Keep still," I said to myself, "stand upright – back and across." Les Lenham years earlier had taught me how to face fast bowlers. Strangely enough I wasn't scared. In many ways I preferred facing Marshall to the medium pace of Tremlett who was bowling at the other end. I left him to Imran. He didn't mind.

So back and across I went. Marshall's arm came over high and fast. Simultaneously I heard a thud as the ball hit the pitch just short of a length. I sensed it was rearing up towards my chest. Uncertainly I fended at it. The ball passed by my side without causing harm but, as it did so, just brushed my glove on its way through to Hampshire's wicket-keeper, Bobby Parks.

After a short pause the Hampshire fielders (Parks, Pocock, Nicholas, Greenidge, Jesty) and the bowler bellowed out their loud appeal, the outcome of which was, to their eyes, bound to be successful.

I had in the process of playing my shot, at best a feeble prod to leg, turned in the direction of Parks' diving glove and Eastbourne's large town hall clock, whose bongs boomed out every fifteen minutes. I saw the catch cleanly taken and yet remained glued to the crease amidst much noise from the opposition. I knew the ball had grazed the side of my glove, and the Hampshire close fielders and bowler knew it too. And yet I stood there in defiance of the evidence.

The umpire at the bowler's end was David Shepherd. He had been a most popular cricketer, a middle-order batsman with Gloucestershire in his playing days. Somewhat stout in stature he became a first-class umpire in 1981 and immediately fitted the bill and warmed to the task. We all liked and respected him. Indeed, in the late 1970s I had sat with him behind the bowler's arm in the pavilion at Bristol and encouraged him to pursue an umpiring career. Subsequently he took the exams, started with some second team and university matches and never looked back. I stood at the crease stubbornly in front of a man I trusted and who, up till now, trusted me. It was a bad moment.

After a pause and having given time for consideration, Shepherd said, "Not out". Marshall expected players to 'walk' when he was bowling and, for the most part, they did so obligingly, preferring the comfort of the pavilion to the battleground at the crease. Amidst the confusion Shepherd called "Over" which helped remove the tension for a moment.

I wandered down the pitch to greet my partner Imran who grinned at me. "A brave thing to do, Johnny," he said, followed by, "I think I had better get down that end next over." It was a generous gesture and one which I was happy to go along with. I felt this was a moment when an overseas player could truly show his worth.

I returned to the non-striker's end and, as I did so, Nick Pocock, the Hampshire captain, strolled past me. "Did you hit that one?" he asked. "I'm afraid to say I did," I replied sheepishly and with shame in my voice. "I thought so," he said and left it at that. Except that he didn't. During the next over, bowled by Tremlett, he relayed a message to Marshall at deep fine leg outlining the gist of his brief conversation with me. By the time Tremlett's over came to an end Marshall's mood had darkened.

The good thing about the next over to be bowled by Marshall was that I wasn't facing it. Imran and I had contrived to swap ends. After all, he had just reached his hundred and was our senior overseas player and, I expect, he got paid more than I did too. But he was happy to take the flak and did so uncomplainingly, even with the suggestion of a smile on his face.

At the non-striker's end I was fidgeting about, feeling embarrassed. I hated incidents at the best of times and particularly when they involved me. With my head bowed I attempted to tender my apologies to Shepherd. "All part of the job, my lad," was all he said. I felt uncomfortable and slightly sick. What made matters even worse was that the crowd, ever loyal to the home captain, had rather taken my side and saw Marshall as the evil-doer of this confrontation.

Amidst my anxiety the game continued with Marshall running in as fast as ever to bowl at Imran. When he reached the crease something unforeseen occurred. As he prepared to bowl, he stopped suddenly; no mean feat given his acceleration, and whipped off the bails at the bowler's end. He appealed loudly as I had drifted absent-mindedly and unenthusiastically out of my ground, not in the least bit wishing to get down the other end. "Howzat," he bellowed, glaring at me and Shepherd and the crease more or less simultaneously. Shepherd was startled and looked a little non-plussed. I think he asked Marshall whether he wished the appeal to stand. "You'll have to give me out," I said, turning to Shepherd. "Indeed I think I will," he replied and raised his finger as the umpire's symbol of execution.

I made my way slowly back to the pavilion and was aware of a few boos emanating from the normally serene Saffrons crowd. I was about half-way there when Pocock, the Hampshire captain, came running over from his position at slip shouting, "No, no, no, we don't play cricket like that in Hampshire. If it's all right, Shep, I'd like to withdraw the appeal."

At this stage I was more than happy to be out; in fact it was a merciful release from the hostile ordeal. "Don't worry about me," I shouted to Pocock, "I'm happy to go quietly." The upshot of these shenanigans was that I was given a reprieve and had to return to the non-striker's end to continue the battle. Marshall finished the over without further incident, so far as I can remember, but at the end of it he hurled the ball fiercely at Pocock and declared he would do no more bowling.

Imran, never one to miss out on a bit of fun, came down to talk to me at the end of the over and said, "Johnny, that's a fine way to see off the country's leading fast bowler." For a moment, despite my shame, I felt I had done something to ease the pain.

So Marshall, who was comfortably the most successful bowler playing county cricket at the time, had banished himself to the boundary in something of a sulk. Someone had to bowl instead and the lot fell to Trevor Jesty. Jesty bowled relatively tempting away swingers at gentle pace and, by comparison with Marshall, was a joy to see holding the ball. Imran certainly thought so. It took just three balls for him to lose his head completely and fall to a jubilant Jesty, bowled middle stump.

Imran's hundred was a bonus. He shouldn't really have been playing at all. Earlier in the summer he had been diagnosed with shin soreness, stress fractures ominously revealing themselves. His surgeon told him he could bat if he was careful – not easy – and bowl a maximum of four overs a day to stimulate growth in the bones. This procedure seemed to me unusual, and I had my doubts as a layman whether this would accelerate healing.

On the other hand it was quite a challenge to have a stab at introducing Imran into the attack so as to make best use of such slender rations and optimise our chance of success. There was one occasion when we got it dead right.

The match was played later in August that same year against Warwickshire at Edgbaston. Kallicharran and Amiss were batting with assured serenity in Warwickshire's second innings when all of a sudden, after a partnership of 135, Amiss fell lbw to Colin Wells. After consultation with Imran, between us we decided it was his moment to bowl his four overs. In fact, as it turned out, I over-bowled him; he had three extra balls into his fifth over. His spell could only be described as a success. In 27 balls he took six wickets for six runs, all bowled or lbw. Off just four paces he swung the ball, like a sparrow-hawk in flight, prodigiously and at speed.

The Warwickshire batsmen just couldn't cope with the movement. Whether or not Imran's surgeon was pleased with this activity has remained unknown, but the shins did recover in due course and Imran returned eventually to his full run-up. But he never again bowled so devastatingly as this, and with an old ball too, which had seen better days. Despite these heroics Warwickshire went on to win the match by 21 runs.

And so back to Marshall and Hampshire. Marshall was one of the best cricketers and certainly the most complete bowler I ever played against. He combined stamina with control and could swing the ball both ways at pace with a surprisingly open-chested bowling action. Not being particularly tall he was ideally built for long, unyielding spells. Unlike many he didn't hold himself back in county matches, and he was effective from both round and over the wicket. He made the batsman play, and precious little went down the leg side (save my nudge to Bobby Parks). He had considerable self-confidence and composure. In short he was a handful to face and one who struck fear into many a batsmen. Marshall was a clever bowler with a good brain.

Strangely enough, though, I had always felt more comfortable against pace than anything else. I trusted my technique. Back and across, into line, head still and hands high. Normally this stood me in good stead despite being undone by Marshall at Eastbourne. In the end that day he did get me, caught brilliantly one-handed in the gulley by Gordon Greenidge. He deserved that wicket, for I had treated him badly and lost a bit of honour too.

Imran was undoubtedly a magnificent all-rounder as well and an intriguing person to have in the Sussex side but, if I could have had first pick of all the overseas players in county cricket at that time, I think I would have chosen Malcolm Marshall. He was a truly great cricketer and a very friendly chap too – off the field.

Raymond Illingworth

Born: Pudsey, Yorkshire, 8 June 1932

61 Tests for England (1958-73)

1,836 runs at an average of 23.24, 2 centuries

122 wickets at an average of 31.20

31 Tests as captain

787 first-class matches (1951-1983)

24,134 runs at an average of 28.06, 22 centuries

2,072 wickets at an average of 20.27

Ray Illingworth made his debut as a 19-year-old in 1951, and he played for the last time in 1983 at the age of 51. With 787 first-class and 218 one-day matches, he has notched up more playing days than almost any other post-war cricketer.

A wily off-break bowler and useful batsman, he was a vital member of the Yorkshire side that won seven championships between 1959 and 1968, but it was his move to Leicestershire, sparked by a contract dispute, that proved the making of him. He was appointed captain, winning the county five trophies – their first ever, including the championship — in his ten years at the helm.

Within weeks of joining Leicestershire in 1969, he became England captain, and his start-stop Test career blossomed. In 1970/71 his side won the Ashes in Australia without losing a Test – he is the only England captain to have achieved this since 1888 – and without his bowlers being awarded a single lbw decision in six long Tests.

In 1982, back at Yorkshire as manager, he led the county to the Sunday League title. Then, after a spell as a television commentator, he became England's cricketing supremo – chairman of selectors and team manager – in 1994.

Ray Illingworth

England's World Cup campaign early in 1996 was not its finest hour nor did it ever come near to being so. It was pounced upon us hard on the heels of an epic Test series against South Africa, with hardly time to recover before we flew east to compete in the one-day tournament on grounds in India and Pakistan. It was to have been Sri Lanka too, but an exploding bomb put paid to that.

Preparations for the World Cup had already begun in South Africa where we had played a series of seven consecutive one-day matches, mostly ignominiously. The squad and indeed its team manager, Ray Illingworth, were full of hope that these failures might represent a good omen for the future, believing that to peak too early would take the wind out of our sails before we really got down to business. But as John Cleese said in his film *Clockwise*, "I can take the despair; it's just the hope I can't stand."

In the event we never quite got into our stride despite recording minor triumphs in Peshawar against Holland and the United Arab Emirates. New Zealand narrowly beat us in Ahmedabad, and South Africa thrashed us in Rawalpindi. We wobbled along precariously but still looked as though we might just qualify for the quarter-finals. However badly we played, it still looked as if we were going to make the cut.

Our final group match was played early in March against Pakistan in Karachi in hot, sultry weather. I remember before the game Illingworth told me he had received a call from a bookmaker. "What did you say to him?" I asked. He smiled wryly and said he told him to fuck off. How could he possibly have predicted anything about England anyway?

The outcome of the game wasn't as bad as it might have been. True, we did lose, but we showed just a little more style in doing so. Indeed, for brief moments in the match, there were glimmers of hope. Javed Miandad, playing in possibly his last major match in front of a home crowd, led out the Pakistan team. It was years since we had played together at Sussex, but he still saw me as a long-lost friend, presumably because many of his friends had been lost forever over the years.

After the match, which was concluded late at night, we traipsed back to the Pearl Continental Hotel to recover – tired, sweaty, dusty and much in need of a soothing bath. The encouraging news was that, despite only having beaten Holland and the United Arab Emirates, we were proceeding to the knock-out stages of the tournament.

Back at the hotel, at least along my corridor which was dimly lit and smelt slightly of damp carpets, guards were stationed at each end of the passage with guns at the ready. This was all part of a complex plan to ensure our safety. Room doors were left open to avoid any sense of loneliness after defeat, and baths were being run. Up and down the corridor there was much chat and banter while the guards looked on, clearly startled by English eccentricity in the face of adversity.

Out of the blue the composure of the night was shattered by a loud howl from Illingworth who, in his enthusiasm to take a dip in the bath tub, had plunged his left foot in without taking the precaution to test the water first. Unfortunately they do hot water very well in Pakistan. He quickly withdrew his scalded foot from the water and hopped up and down the corridor, swearing loudly and fiercely.

The guards, presuming an unwanted intruder had disturbed Illingworth, ran down the passage wielding their guns while Illy jumped about in agony, dressed only in a skimpy, fluffy white towel. It wasn't a great sight to behold. It came as something of a shock to Muslim guards not used to seeing the human frame so scantily clad.

What with the commotion and Illy's ranting, it had gone unnoticed that water was still pouring from the tap and into the bath and over the edge. It was just beginning to seep into the room. All efforts to turn off the tap were in vain. It was stuck; boiling water was beginning to spread ominously towards Illingworth's belongings which were hastily being moved to higher ground. Despite the late hour, maintenance was called and spanners emerged from tool kits to stem the flow and avert disaster. Total crisis, such as evacuation from the hotel, was averted.

Players, and indeed Illingworth himself, returned to their rooms and turned out the lights after another unpredictable day in Pakistan. At this stage of the campaign I think it would be fair to say that things were not proceeding with noticeable harmony either on or off the field.

It did not take long for Illingworth's foot to recover, albeit amidst some grumbling, and Sri Lanka gave us a hiding at Faisalabad in the quarter-finals where Jayasuriya turned the one-day game on its head with a display of assertive batting, the like of which I had not seen before. So our campaign had completely run out of steam, and we returned in mid-March to daffodils and primroses in England, relieved to be home.

I think it would not be unkind to say that Illingworth's career as a coach, manager and indeed, chairman of selectors, was not a patch on the span of years he spent as a player – batsman, bowler and captain – at Yorkshire, Leicestershire and, of course, for England. He was absolutely in his element when he was actually plying his trade on the field as opposed to when he was watching from off it, with little more than hope to comfort him. As a captain he was, without doubt, one of the best since the war, rivalled, I suppose, only by Brearley whose style was so different it is hard to compare them.

Illingworth was very shrewd, a thinker, something of a schemer but always alert to the needs of the team and, like Brearley, there was a certain edginess to his demeanour – not a man with whom to trifle. Possibly he was at his best when up against it. He measured that subtle balance between attack and defence with great dexterity. Brearley was good at this, too, but Tony Greig not so, veering frequently from wild excesses of offence to all-out defence within a couple of overs. However, Greig was blessed with quite different and endearing traits of leadership to make up for this. It was said by many that Illingworth preferred only to bowl himself when conditions were helpful. This may have been true to some extent, but never forget that the pressure is on in such circumstances and expectations high. Without doubt Illingworth absorbed pressure well and added to this the blessing of patience.

As a youngster I was weak against spin and had yet to establish a technique to combat flight and guile. Illingworth was as hard as any I had to face, never unplayable as Underwood could be on a wet pitch, but unnervingly accurate and with teasing variations. I simply couldn't get him away; just a quick single would occasionally have been handy so as to escape to the other end. But no, the line and length were always menacing, and it made me feel sick. The likes of Titmus, Pocock, Birkenshaw and, later, Edmonds and Emburey were also very skilful, but at least they dropped their guard occasionally to allow a run to be scored. I hated Illingworth; his bowling, that is; he trotted in gently, silent always, craggy and with wily thoughts permeating his brain. It was no fun at all.

Illingworth didn't miss a trick. I vividly recall the successful outcome of the final Test match at Sydney in February 1971 when England regained the Ashes. I was lying in bed at school listening to my transistor radio concealed beneath the pillow – thousands of others must have been doing the same – as events unfolded on the final morning. Australia, you may remember, were within striking distance of winning the match and squaring the series and so had to be bowled out. Nothing could have been more tense; every ball mattered; the field had to be placed with great precision; a single mistake could be fatal. Nobody in the world could have been more in his element than Illingworth. He was both ruthless in his outlook, composed in his disposition and lethally effective. He bowled, so far as I can remember, for most of the morning and winkled out three Australian batsmen, including the dangerous Greg Chappell. Underwood helped him out too, and it was the unlikely presence of D'Oliveira who did the trick towards the end, another calm man well used to the whole rigmarole of crisis. But it was really Illingworth who masterminded the victory and the Ashes success, not so much with the finesse of a diplomatic statesman but more with the simple down-to-earth blood and guts of a professional who knew his craft through and through. He was very, very much a Yorkshireman and with a keen brain to run alongside this background.

In May one year in the 1970s we travelled to Leicester to play a championship match. It was cold and cheerless, and nobody much had bothered to turn up to watch – a standard day, in fact. Grace Road could be bleak and uninviting in such conditions. I got out early, possibly to McKenzie or Higgs, and so when, later, Illingworth came on to bowl I sat myself on the very top of the pavilion, looking out over the ground to see if I could learn something from the master. Despite the weather he couldn't be doing with much of a warm-up – a roll of the shoulders and a couple of turns of the hips was about all he went in for – he set the field meticulously and then, ball after ball, proceeded to trot in, quite a long run-up, to bowl with a comfortable and fluent action. Despite the cold he bowled with his sleeves rolled up, a 'no-nonsense' look, and took his sweater politely from the umpire at the end of each over, doubtless chatting him up a little at the same time. He may have bowled a half-volley or two to Tony Greig who, with his long reach, drove the ball through the covers for four, but he remained unfazed, icy cool, and continued his spell with the confidence of a man who will ultimately be rewarded for his labour. He bowled over the wicket to the right-handers from close to the stumps, drifting the ball a touch from leg to off. Under the new decision review system he would have accounted for more victims by the hundreds. Sussex batsmen were never very clever when playing Illingworth on the slower pitches of the Midlands and North.

But Illingworth was not perfect, far from it. He could get angry and occasionally showed his teeth. In that same match at Leicester I first came across David Gower. Eighteen years old with lots of curly fair hair, he floated out to bat ghost-like and then proceeded to caress the ball elegantly around Grace Road's large outfield. That he was a pretty player to watch must have been all the more irritating to his captain who was more used to seeing cricketers graft their way into first-class cricket on the battlefields of Sheffield and Bradford. Gower was something of a misfit in that Leicester side of the mid-seventies for whom Duddleston, John Steele, Balderstone and Davison were the main run scorers.

Gower batted both pleasingly and effortlessly on that cold Leicester morning, during which I watched his progress towards an impressive half-century with growing envy. Shortly before lunch I was called upon to bowl, more in desperation than hope, and Gower, both casually and obligingly, hit my third ball straight to mid-on where Michael Buss took the catch. A minor triumph which brought Gower's captain, Illingworth, to the crease. All the way to the wicket I could hear him muttering and moaning beneath his breath. "Fucking young pup, getting out like that," he chuntered. "He's gone and spoilt my fucking lunch." When he set his mind to it Illingworth could win gold medals for incessant grumbling. If he dropped his toast on the floor, you could be sure it would never land butter side up and, even if it did, he would still tend to look on the downside. I have a dim recollection, some twenty years later, of Shirley, his wife, unluckily losing her luggage in Durban. "I can handle the inconvenience," Illy stoically said to me, "but I fear she will begin to smell." It was very vexing.

Rarely did Illingworth miss a trick either on the cricket field or when playing bridge, which he loved to do when nothing much else was going on. In South Africa in 1995/96 he played golf and bridge whenever the opportunity arose and so, in this way, would escape from the daily grind of cricket and recharge the batteries. His usual bridge partners were Philip Bell, the team doctor, Malcolm Ashton, scorer and my valiant accounting assistant (in fact, he did the job for me), and Mike Atherton whom I soon discovered could turn his hand to pretty well anything and be good at it. Just occasionally one of these was for whatever reason unavailable so I made up the numbers.

Hitherto I had only ever played some very informal family bridge. So I just about knew the basics but no more. I always partnered Illingworth who was unimpressed by my style. "Two rather wobbly spades," I would bid somewhat timidly. He would fix me with a cold stare. And then there was always the post-mortem after each hand during which my technique, tactics and ignorance were exposed in a humiliating burst of wrath – mostly tongue in cheek, I must admit, but wounding nonetheless.

Illingworth did rather let me off the hook on the field at Hove one day, allowing me to breathe more freely than should have been the case. I was returning to the Sussex side somewhat prematurely having broken my thumb at Portsmouth only four weeks earlier. I was determined in a rather foolhardy fashion to play and declared myself fit without any practice less than an hour before the match. Despite all this I played for me with rare dash and bravado in this my come-back game against Leicestershire. I took it into my head, I think for the first and last time in my career, that I could play the hook shot which I did persistently and with remarkably good effect against Paddy Clift, Peter Booth (my schoolboy cricket-touring friend) and Les Taylor. They must have felt very embarrassed and humiliated to be buffeted about by me, a confirmed blocker at the best of times. Anyway, the long and short of it was that I raced (by my standards) to 94, 70 of which were scored in a golden two hours before lunch. The most extraordinary thing about all this was that Illingworth, Leicestershire's captain, never bowled himself, a tactic which would have been much feared by me. His presence with the ball had a mesmeric effect. Doubtless the tinge of green in the pitch had put him off; he felt the seamers should do the job for him. John Steele bowled some spin and Chris Balderstone too, but they were not in the same class as the cunning old fox himself. He let me get away with it which, for a man of his astuteness, was a rare mistake, for which I have always been enormously grateful.

Illingworth was by then getting on a bit, but this wasn't my final match against him. No, he popped up again five years later playing, probably in his fiftieth year, for Yorkshire at Headingley. Not only was he playing, he was for some reason captain. I can't quite remember why, but I think it must have had something to do with Boycott. The match itself was a low-scoring affair played on a slow pitch in front of a good July crowd, and once again Illingworth trundled in to bowl at me. He emerged out of the dark background of the football stand and seemed to deliver the ball with a slower and more deceptive arc than in years gone by. I imagine his back was not quite so strong. Anyway I still struggled to play him with authority. He made the ball dip and bounce, as in the past, accompanied by the running commentary of my friend David Bairstow from behind the stumps. I found the whole ordeal quite a handful before surrendering at the other end to another wily chap, Phil Carrick.

Make no mistake, Illingworth was a very good cricketer, not elegant, a bit stiff in some ways especially when batting, old-fashioned, too, but more, I would say, from the old school which is rather different. Above all else he was a very effective operator, calculating and measured, and blest with Yorkshire self-confidence. "Wasn't Chris Balderstone quite a useful spinner?" I asked him once. "Aye, lad, Baldy were all right, but didn't spin it as much as me." To be fair, most conversations returned to Illingworth; that was just the nature of things.

It was in 1995, some twelve years later, that I rediscovered Illingworth when he had taken over the management of the England team. I was invited by Alan Smith, chief executive of the Test and County Cricket Board, to spend the winter in South Africa as Ray's assistant manager and to follow this up with the World Cup in India and Pakistan. I didn't take much persuading. It was like winning a prize in a raffle; it was a challenge that just couldn't be ignored.

I hastily unravelled and delegated my Arundel duties for that winter. There wasn't much time for pre-tour preparation as we set off less than a month after the 1995 English season had ended. It was for the most part a matter of meeting up with the squad at Heathrow and hoping for the best. Time spent before departure was not entirely wasted: a mass of autographs to be signed, interviews with the loitering press plus weeping wives and girlfriends saying fond farewells to be consoled. Then, thank God, we were off. Bonding, if you can call it that, was saved for the thirteen-hour flight to Johannesburg where we were warmly welcomed by Mandela's new South Africa and Ali Bacher.

To assist him with the coaching Illingworth brought with him two of his veterans from the 1970 campaign to Australia, John Edrich to look after the batsman and Peter Lever the bowlers. I think Illingworth realised that, for all his experience, he was not a natural coach. Like many others he found it hard to control events on the field without being in the thick of it himself. Instinctively players did not like to confide in him and thus expose their frailties to the man whose prime task was to select the Test team. For example, no one was likely to own up to problems with coping with the mysterious South African spinner Paul Adams when he appeared on the scene.

Edrich and Lever may have taken the pressure off Illingworth for a while, but they only stayed in South Africa for the early part of the tour. We did however have with us, very much on the periphery of the squad, an outsider who had considerable influence and gave some pastoral comfort to several of the players, Andrew Wingfield Digby. As a Christian minister he became, above all, a friend to whom players would chat and maybe occasionally let off steam.

There was nothing official about Andrew's position; he had never been appointed by the Test and County Cricket Board. But he was a useful and secure ally to whom the players could talk. However, Illingworth didn't welcome his presence as others had done before. He was suspicious and didn't really understand the point of him, believing quite firmly that Test players didn't need a shoulder to cry on. He banished Wingfield Digby from the party, which led the players to joke that the England team no longer needed a messenger around the dressing room now that they had the real thing in Illingworth.

While Illingworth set about his business, well respected if slightly feared, Edrich and Lever had to fulfil a more difficult task as coaches. The greatest flaw in coaches and coaching is that those employed feel they actually have to do something to justify their position. Unluckily this was the case, to some extent, in South Africa. In bridge terms it was very much hoped that Devon Malcolm might be a trump card. He had the ability and physique to bowl very fast and perhaps complement Angus Fraser's more classical style. But Malcolm's bowling was undeniably a bit wild and erratic, and Lever made well-meaning attempts to smooth things out in his action. Assuming that this is akin to altering a golf swing in mid-tournament, it was a high-risk tactic which just might have worked but would more likely confuse the athlete who would not want too many thoughts of technique swilling about in his brain.

The outcome was not a success. Malcolm, despite much practice and effort, was not selected for the first Test match at Centurion Park in conditions which might have suited him. In the event it rained, but I fear it was still a blow to his confidence. He did play in the second Test at the Wanderers in Johannesburg, when Atherton saved the day, and with some success, too, taking six wickets in the match. For some reason he didn't play in Durban or Port Elizabeth, and then came that ill-fated match in Cape Town when the clouds finally burst and all hell let loose.

Illingworth was not always easy to read; he would often talk when you might prefer him to be quiet and be quiet when you wanted him to talk. 'Sunny' would not be the word to describe his normal disposition, and yet he disguised his inherent Yorkshire dourness with a calm and composed countenance, accompanied occasionally with a twinkle of humour. Malcolm touched a raw spot, though, and Illingworth was unable to contain his frustration. Malcolm had undoubtedly got it in him to do what Snow had done in Australia twenty-five years earlier. He had pace but perhaps not quite the class to go with it, and this brought out the darker side of Illingworth's character. It exposed a fierce temper which took some of us by surprise.

The Test match at Newlands in Cape Town was played on a slowish pitch of uneven bounce. Neither side coped well. England collapsed in its first innings for 153, and South Africa in reply floundered, too, at 171 for nine before 18-year-old Paul Adams, famous for his weird bowling action purveying googlies and chinamen, joined the experienced David Richardson at the crease. In a chaotic hour or so they flayed about, with luck and skill, to such an extent that 73 more runs were added to the score. It was, I suppose, the moment when Malcolm should have wrapped things up and at least given England a chance of winning the match. In the event nobody bowled very well, including poor Malcolm, for whom it seemed the harder he tried the worse things got. It was one of those ghastly sessions which happen occasionally, and it was poorly timed.

South Africa as a result got away from us and Illingworth, watching from the stand, began to simmer. The kettle was on the boil, and by the time Adams was finally out he stormed into the dressing room and blew his top. He could bear it no more and bombarded the weary and dejected Malcolm with a stream of abuse which only a mixture of pent-up frustration and anger could possibly produce. With temper, things often get said which the perpetrator regrets, and Illingworth was not proud of this tirade. It was not really his style, but he just could not help himself in the heated atmosphere produced by the potent mixture of disappointment and failure. There is nothing like wounded pride to bring the worst out of people.

The storm was over in a trice. Flashes of lightning and thunder were replaced by the sound of ripping velcro as Stewart and Atherton strapped on their pads for the second innings. Neither were successful, nor was the rest of the team which for the second time in the match had no answer to the undoubted talent and pace of Donald and Pollock.

Failure did not sit easily with Illingworth; it doesn't do so readily with anyone, and he certainly wasn't used to it. Brought up in the hard and unyielding school of Yorkshire cricket where favours are granted to no one, Illingworth in his prime developed and cultivated the finest cricket brain of his generation: shrewd, thoughtful and very skilful. To be manager of the England team combined with responsibilities as chairman of selectors was too much to ask of him and came too late in his career. To negotiate both the hurdles of Test and one-day cricket was at the time more than anyone could have handled successfully. Only Illingworth's innate Yorkshire pride stood in his way; with hindsight it was a bridge too far and badly thought out.

I value my friendship and relationship with Illingworth; my life would be a great deal poorer for its absence. In many ways we could not be more different in background, approach and thinking. Yet I noticed that neither of us liked to give anything away or give any quarter for that matter; sort of ruthless in a way.

Both of us tend to bang on when it comes to cricket or anything else for that matter and sometimes drive our audience into submission. Illingworth talks a lot at times, mostly about himself and distant triumphs, which is fun for a bit. I'm afraid I do the same occasionally but have a lot less to talk about.

Ian James Gould

Born: Taplow, Buckinghamshire, 19 August 1957

298 first-class matches (1975-1996)
8,756 runs at an average of 26.05, 4 centuries

536 catches and 67 stumpings

Ian Gould is the longest-serving English umpire on the International Cricket Council's Elite Panel, to which he was appointed in 2009. As such he stands in Test matches all round the world.

As a player, for Middlesex and Sussex, he was an attacking left-handed batsman and a highly talented wicket-keeper, playing for England in 18 one-day internationals including the World Cup of 1983.

His move from Middlesex to Sussex in 1981 coincided with a rise in the fortunes of the South Coast county, and during 1986 he stood in as captain for much of the summer, leading Sussex to victory in the NatWest final at Lord's. His appointment for the following summer was less successful, though he did end his reign with a thrilling 88-ball century against Northamptonshire at Hove. Curiously his three hundreds for Sussex – in 1985, 1987 and 1989 – were all scored in the final match of the summer at Hove.

He became a first-class umpire in 2002, following ten years of coaching at Middlesex.

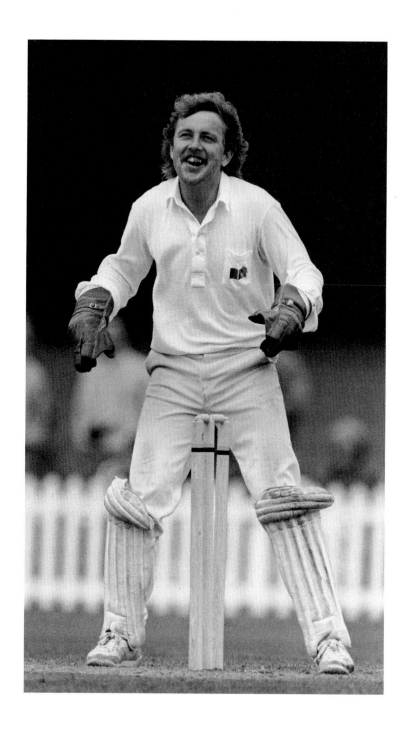

Ian Gould

It had been a long day, and we had been in the field for most of it. Our enchantment with the game was just beginning to wear a little thin. I was fielding at second slip, as I usually did, and Gould was keeping wicket, of course. "Cheer up, skip," he said to me. "We're the lucky ones. Just think – we could be umpiring." There was a silence during which a few more balls were bowled and nothing happened. The umpire in question just could have been Sam Cook, the former Gloucester slow bowler with whom Gould would share fags and a light. "I could no more become an umpire than dance in the music hall," Gould confided to me as we crossed for a new over. "Boring, exhausting – and all that concentration. No, not for me. Never."

I first came across Gould when, aged 15, he joined the MCC Young Cricketers and, under the watchful eyes of Len Muncer and Harry Sharp, began to shape his game. He made a hundred for them at Hove in 1972, and it wasn't long before Don Bennett, the Middlesex coach, snapped him up and invited him to join the Middlesex professional staff along with Mike Gatting. Gatting and Gould were the two rising stars at Lord's in the early seventies, and there was much talk of their potential. Gould was indeed quite an all-rounder; not only was he quickly shaping up as a promising wicket-keeper/batsman but he was also for a while on the Arsenal's books as a budding young goalkeeper when Bob Wilson was still in his heyday as senior keeper. Gould was certainly agile enough, confident and noisy, but considered just short of an inch or two in height for top-class goalkeeping. So he had to settle for the more modest life-style of cricket for which he turned out to be very well suited.

There is little doubt that Gould enjoyed his life within the close-knit family of professional cricket. He was a natural, born with a precocious gift to hit the ball cleanly. He had fun as well, too much for some, but there lay the essence of his character. He much enjoyed a social drink and would happily unwind after a hard day with some liquid refreshment; he was rarely short of friends to fill his glass. Benson and Hedges and John Player sponsored two of the four competitions so he was never short of fags either, which he would dish out as generously as he would smoke them. I should say he was lucky to play in an era when a cup of tea, a cheese roll and a cigarette constituted a warm-up for the day's play. As a result his figure tended towards slight roundness as indeed did Gatting's although, of the two, I should have said that Gatting just about held the aces when it came to organisation and professionalism. As for talent there wasn't much in it. Both had sparkle and flair.

By 1977 Gould was pretty well established in the Middlesex side, and by 1980 he was keeping wicket to just about the strongest county bowling attack imaginable: Daniel, van der Bijl, Selvey, Edmonds and Emburey and even a little bit of Titmus who was drafted in for a match or two. But despite this all was not well. Paul Downton had been recruited to Middlesex from Kent where Alan Knott still reigned supreme. So the presence of Gould and Downton in the wicket-keeping department made for a bit of a squash at Lord's. Something had to give. Gould joined Sussex for the 1981 season. One way or another, bearing in mind his ability, Gould had rather under-achieved at Middlesex so we were all full of hope that the switch out of London down to the coast might do the trick – and indeed it did.

It didn't take long for me as his new captain to get to know him. For a start he talked even more than I did, though the accent I'm told differed somewhat. He chatted when he batted; he chatted behind the stumps; he chatted in the dressing room. Possibly to some extent the result of nerves. He was mates with everyone. Almost instantly he was dominant with the bat, didn't miss much behind the stumps and was helpful tactically. He was observant and knew all the opposition players well and so was in close touch with their strengths and weaknesses. In that first season he was the country's leading keeper with 59 catches and four stumpings. It helped to bring us within a whisker of winning the County Championship.

So far as I was concerned Gould was a cockney who spoke with a rich London dialect and educated all of us and especially Imran Khan in the finer points of cockney rhyming slang. "The plates are 'umming and there's a bit of a ding-dong in 'ere, stiff Gregory too and where are me mums." A lot more nonsense, too. In actual fact Gould was not a Londoner; he came from Slough just west of the city and only separated from Eton College by the passage of the M4 which sweeps as a boundary between the two. In 1981 we played the Minor Counties in an early Benson and Hedges match at Slough. For much of the time it rained so I took some of the team, including Gould, over to visit my old school. When we had tired of sightseeing our minds turned to food and I knew just the place, 'The Cockpit' in the High Street, which served traditional teas – hot buttered toast, scones and cream and poached eggs. "What? Flippin' poached eggs," Gould muttered in disbelief and put it down to Etonian eccentricity before tucking in.

Gould was without doubt a character and a strong one, too. Not wishing to sound too old-fashioned, there was probably more room thirty years ago for these unexpected traits of personality within professional cricket. Life had yet to be ruled by i-pod, i-pad, i-phone and all manner of computer-generated activity. Television was prominent, of course, but that was about it. So Gould was a communicator, an incessant talker, with lots of friends scattered throughout the country. He knew about people and came to understand them better and better. He was an invaluable scout and source of information about our opponents. He seemed to know how so many of them ticked.

I think it was Geoff Arnold who spotted his immense potential for our team before I did. In preparation for the 1981 season I took the whole squad for a weekend get-together based at a hotel near Chichester. (Dubai hadn't really become prominent at this stage.) Here we plotted our season's campaign, and Arnold came up with the very positive idea that Gould, as a left-hander of course, should open the batting in one-day cricket – the first of the pinch-hitters, if you like, although that expression was still a long way off being coined. "Let's make really good use of our new acquisition," was Arnold's view. And so we did, to great effect.

Gould formed an outstanding partnership with Gehan Mendis, and it wasn't until we played Worcestershire in June that we lost a match. All was going well that day until six o'clock when the bells of St Mary's Church, Horsham began to ring out loudly to signify Evensong. These bells are indeed beautiful and much appreciated by a congregation beckoned to church in the evening sunshine. Despite this idyllic English scene, the volume of the bells and the length of their peal played havoc with my field setting. The problem was that no one could hear my instructions as I bellowed them out over the ground. Fielders became confused and flustered, and out of the blue the Worcestershire late order began to get on top. John Inchmore, more famous as a fast bowler than batsman, was the problem. He kept slapping the ball away on the leg-side, evading our fielders who, surprisingly, were predominantly placed on the off-side. It was a poor piece of captaincy. Tony Pigott was the unlucky bowler who suffered most, but it could have been anyone and the outcome of it all was that Worcester scored more than 50 in the last four overs to win the game. When it was all over, back in the pavilion we were a bit downcast and silent. Imran, who had formerly played for Worcestershire, broke this period of gloom. "Inchers only has one shot," he said. "The slog to leg." Gould who was sitting silently in a corner retorted in colourful language: "Well thanks for the tip – bit late now." That was the gist of it, anyway.

It wasn't just the runs that Gould scored in this new elevated position but the spirit he gave to it. He seemed to thrive on the extra responsibility which was not just confined to one-day cricket. We played in a three-day championship match against Kent at Tunbridge Wells which all of a sudden and quite unexpectedly brought out the best in him. It was a match in June, rhododendrons resplendent, which had, for more than two and a half days, done little to stir the spirits of the spectators in the marquees which surrounded the ground. Asif Iqbal, Kent's captain, had rather let me down by failing to declare Kent's second innings which laboured on into the early evening with Taylor and Tavaré accumulating easy runs against the spin of Barclay and Waller. Just when it seemed that Asif would allow this funereal dirge to run its course, he made what then would have been considered a 'token' declaration, inviting Sussex to score 228 runs in 25 overs. As I was strapping on my pads in the dank and dingy dressing room, sunk beneath the pavilion and with few, if any, redeeming features – a hard stone floor and only one loo, hopelessly inadequate for professional cricketers, I was awakened from my uncomfortable nightmare by a shout, "Why don't we go for 'em, give 'em a shock?" Gould was backed up in this fool-hardy suggestion by Parker and Phillipson who were plainly bored and fancied a bit of action. Flexibility always nestling at the heart of captaincy, we instantly changed gear and gave ourselves two minutes to work out some tactics to accompany our enthusiasm. Gould and Mendis opened the batting and in less than five overs brought up the fifty. Kent were visibly shaken, and in no time fielders were scattered about the boundaries, protecting the spectators if nothing else. Gould made a dazzling 28, Mendis continued to play the innings of his life and the others chipped in and for a while kept up the momentum. We pursued the target way beyond the time when good sense and logic should have prevailed and reined us in. Underwood finally did for us by bowling both Mendis and Waller in the final over. I suppose it was something of a glorious defeat. It showed what could be done with committed teamwork and a willing spirit. This match as much as any other firmly established Gould's position within the hearts of all our players. It was a bit of a turning point.

Gould could be very funny, too. Also at Tunbridge Wells but a year or two later, Chris Waller was bowling his left-arm spinners to Christopher Cowdrey in another championship match between Sussex and Kent. Waller tossed the ball up a little higher and Cowdrey, tempted by the flight, danced down the wicket and took the fly, as it were. He struck the ball cleanly but airily in the direction of long-off where Colin Wells, fielding in front of the pavilion, did not have to move to take a comfortable catch. Cowdrey was livid with himself and, uttering a couple of seasoned oaths, swore loudly even before the ball had been caught. Meanwhile Gould who had had a good view of these proceedings from behind the stumps fell upon the ground laughing, kicking his heals in the air wildly. "It wasn't that funny," I suggested. "No, but nothing is more hilarious than a public school toff swearing," he replied as he got up again in preparation for the next batsman.

With my fielding at slip all day and so standing next to Gould, we did a lot of talking – non-stop most of the time. He was a good judge of a player, as I have said, and well aware of the likes and dislikes of the opposition; a subtle piece of field placing or a change of bowling could make all the difference. On one occasion I remember Chris Broad and Tim Robinson opening the batting for Nottinghamshire at Trent Bridge against the pace of Imran Khan and Garth le Roux. This was a fine contest between very good players which I was quietly enjoying from slip when Gould suddenly turned to me and said, "Skip, you've got to bowl." "Me, why me?" I asked. "Because Broad can't play spin." This was an unexpected turn of events but I did as I was told and, grabbing the newish ball in the seventh over, I prepared to bowl to Broad. My first ball slipped a little out of my hand and landed short outside the left-handed Broad's off stump. His eyes lit up, he stepped onto the back foot and slapped the ball straight into the safe hands of Greig at cover point. Out. A wicket. A complete fluke. Randall was the next batsman in, and he played out the rest of the over without further alarm. A maiden over. As I took my sweater from the umpire I heard Gould's chirpy voice in the background. "Well bowled, skip, I think that will do for now." I took myself off and returned contentedly to slip while we reverted to more orthodox tactics.

Without doubt Gould, who was always a Londoner and Lord's man at heart, saw his form and reputation take a great leap forward after joining Sussex and its unusual combination of players. It was, if you like, a second chance for him to display his talent in a dressing room far removed from and probably more relaxed than in those successful Middlesex sides to which he had become accustomed. The result of all this was that he was selected to tour with England in Australia over the winter of 1982/83. It must have been the perfect tour for him. He didn't have to play very much, one or two appearances in the one-day matches against New Zealand and some twelfth man duties which did include a sensational contribution in the extraordinary Boxing Day Test match at Melbourne. Fielding as substitute for Graeme Fowler, Gould caught the catch of his life, diving to his right low down at cover from a Greg Chappell cut off Norman Cowans. It was a stunning moment as well as being acrobatic. How long Gould stayed on the field, I can't remember, but you will recall that the match ended with Australia just four runs short of victory when Botham bowled a short ball to Jeff Thomson who edged it high and hard to Chris Tavaré at second slip. The ball burst through his hands and Geoff Miller nipped nimbly round behind him to complete the catch, save the day and secure England's victory. Despite this valiant effort at Melbourne, it wasn't enough to overcome the Australians who won the series by two Test matches to one.

Gould deservedly kept his place in England's World Cup squad for the tournament played in England in 1983. He kept wicket tidily and scored some useful scampered runs towards the end of the innings without ever perhaps having the opportunity to produce his best form. This interlude with the England team would have been predicted confidently by his Middlesex coach, Don Bennett. Gould and Gatting were undoubtedly his stars, and Gould possibly even the favourite to achieve great things. The story, though, didn't run quite as it should. After all Gould was more a man of flair than application. He didn't belong to the Gooch school of training. Reliability was probably not his strongest attribute. But there was always that chirpy honesty that I found so engaging when chatting to him from slip. He made me laugh. Sometimes that's worth its weight in gold.

By 1986 I was struggling. Depression had reared its snake-like head again, and I was impeded to a lesser extent by a bashed-up finger. I was in no fit state to carry on as captain so I handed over to Gould at least until the end of the season. It was a good decision. It made me feel better, and he injected some much-needed zest into the team, so much so that we gathered momentum for a challenge in the NatWest Bank one-day trophy. At Headingley in the quarter-final we played Yorkshire on a pitch which resembled a jigsaw puzzle. Unsurprisingly it was a surface on which the devil played his part, diverting balls off at all angles and heights. Sussex did well to reach 86 for six before Gould set about the Yorkshire attack and stunned it into submission by his audacity. He played an innings of Bothamesque proportions. In just a few overs Gould turned the game on its head by scoring 88 runs and, when

Yorkshire batted, by taking four catches, too. It was a remarkable performance by a man whose rich talent shone that afternoon in the north. The NatWest form didn't end there. We went on to beat Lancashire in the final at Lord's, undaunted by strong opposition. Tactically sound and on his home territory, Gould handled the match well, got things right on the day and lifted the trophy triumphantly in the evening. "Watch out, Soho," was all I remember him saying at the press conference. It seemed to sum the situation up pretty well.

Not surprisingly Gould was appointed club captain for 1987. But for whatever reason, despite his natural flair for the game, things didn't go to plan. Constrained perhaps by the responsibility that goes with the job and with leading a team that was by now past its best, Gould lost some of his bounce and jauntiness. The team began to struggle and so did Gould. As the immediate past captain I kept well out of it, and it wasn't until I bumped into him by chance at Fontwell races in August that he poured his heart out as we watched the horses go round the paddock.

"It's absolute hell," he confided, "I'm hating it." I listened for a while to this tale of misery. Humour seemed to be a thing of the past. Eventually I said, "Don't do it. It's not meant to be purgatory. It's spoiling the fun." So he stood down honourably at the end of the season, and Paul Parker took up the reins. But at least Gould did give it a go, not an easy task either, especially when combining captaincy with wicket-keeping while instinctively being one of the boys.

Life can be unpredictable, and some things you would just never guess. After retiring from Sussex in 1990, Gould joined his old friend Mike Gatting to take on the challenge of coaching Middlesex County Cricket Club. The club, for some years out of the limelight, was yearning for immediate success to pacify committees and supporters. But cricket doesn't often work like that, and success was not forthcoming. Gatting and Gould departed, not the dream ticket, and so to some extent had to start again. Against all odds Gould weighed up the pros and cons of life and decided to have a look at umpiring. After all he knew the game well and its characters through and through. As a wicket-keeper (David Constant always felt wicket-keepers made good umpires) surely his concentration and judgement would be good; it wasn't a badly paid job so long as he could pass the dreaded exams which would not be easy; he would have to strengthen up a bit on the self-discipline, but I think it probably helps to have erred and strayed a little in the past. Transgressions are more easily understood.

When I now watch him umpiring, he appears completely at ease with the game and with himself. The talking hasn't stopped, but it's now accompanied by an instinctive authority. He always waves to me from the middle, even at Lord's in a Test match between Pakistan and Australia. "Concentrate," I shout back, but he doesn't hear. After the second day of that match in 2010 we ended up in the MCC Committee Room at Lord's, having a drink with the two teams. It was a semi-formal occasion, but we both looked jolly smart. He saw me standing there and, with a laugh and twinkle in his eye, he said, "Well, Johnny, here we are. In the Committee Room at Lord's, you as President and me as Test match umpire. Who would ever have guessed that?"

Peter Michael Roebuck

Born: Oxford, 6 March 1956
Died: Cape Town, South Africa, 12 November 2011

335 first-class matches (1974-1991)
17,558 runs at an average of 37.27, 33 centuries
72 wickets at an average of 49.16

Peter Roebuck was an outstanding county batsman for Somerset. Coming into his prime at the same time as Viv Richards and Ian Botham, he was a key member of the side that brought its first trophies to the West Country county, winning five one-day titles in the years from 1979 to 1983.

He replaced Botham as captain in 1986, a tumultuous year that ended with Richards, Botham and Joel Garner all leaving the club. They were turbulent times for the beleaguered captain but, in that summer and the next, he scored a two-year total of 2,487 first-class runs at an average, 48.76, that was bettered by only one English batsman, Mike Gatting.

He retired from first-class cricket at the close of the 1991 season. The following summer he joined Devon, whom – from 1994 to 1997 – he led to an unprecedented four successive Minor County Championships. He was an inspiring and original captain, still a capable batsman, but he surprised everybody with the effectiveness of his all-sorts bowling. In 1996 he was the leading wicket-taker in the competition.

One of very few first-class cricketers to win an Oxbridge double first (Ed Smith is another), Peter Roebuck became a leading writer on the game, based in Australia and South Africa.

Peter Roebuck

(written some months before he died)

Some thirty years ago Peter wrote his first book, *Slices of Cricket*, in which he included a chapter about me simply entitled 'Trout'. As a relatively humble county cricketer I was flattered by the attention. It was most welcome. A good deal has happened since then, much water has flowed beneath the bridge, so I thought it high time to repay the compliment and write a short piece about Peter.

Peter tells a story of his taking a scholarship to the senior school at Millfield. In the course of interviewing him in his study the headmaster, R.J.O. Meyer, suddenly flicked a tennis ball at Peter who caught it deftly in his right hand. This athletic feat seemed to do the trick and clinch the deal. Peter was admitted as a scholar. Few, though, would dispute that he is a clever chap. You don't get a first at Cambridge for nothing and especially when playing full-time cricket for the university as well.

In the world of county cricket I doubt whether it helps very much to be clever – many days spent in the field, with little to test the brain. In the old days and at Millfield, Peter bowled a few leg breaks but, as length and line began to pass him by, they quickly turned into not very good off-spinners and later seamers. Bowling just could have come to his rescue in the field but, at Somerset, it wasn't to be and he had to content himself with batting, initially at number four. His presence, sandwiched between Viv Richards and Ian Botham, helped out the opposition bowlers a little.

To be fair it can't be easy being clever amidst county cricketers who would instinctively view a big brain with some suspicion. "What was going on in that intellectual head? What plans were being hatched?" In the early days Peter did not always help himself and, unlike Mike Brearley, if we are to make comparisons, stood somewhat aloof from the others. He was perhaps a little shy. Social manner and natural good grace were not his strong points, with the result that he was all too often a little misunderstood. But beneath his clear mind there was always a man of action with a sharp bite. He might indeed have made a good politician if a suitable party could have been found for him. His thick skin and inquiring mind would have taken him a long way. He's a fighter, too.

Peter was a very different chap when he was in your team, on your side. I discovered this when we met up in Sydney, Australia towards the end of 1980. Peter was teaching at Cranbrook School, and I was coaching cricket at Scots College and also playing for Waverley Cricket Club. Peter became a friend. He was an unusual fellow, for sure, but perhaps no more so than me. Never happier than when curled up under a tree with a book, he loved his sport too, ran the Cranbrook first XI, played a lot of tennis (occasionally with me) and also played cricket every now and then for Waverley. I quickly discovered a very different Roebuck, one who was never short of a word or two in the field – mostly about my tactics. He was both funny and fun to have in the team and, although essentially English, he did seem somehow very Australian compared with me and so fitted neatly into the rest of the side.

I was a good old-fashioned blocker. There are not so many of us around now. This amused the Australians and Roebuck too, who were startled when on one occasion I took everyone by surprise in scoring 95 runs in 78 minutes. Peter rushed into the dressing room when it was all over to inquire after my health as such things were surely not meant to be.

Perhaps more significant than our cricket exploits was the legendary Christmas coaching course which we ran together at Scots College during the long summer holiday. Hundreds of children aged between five and thirteen took part, wearing shorts, t-shirts and hats (it was very hot). It became quite a festival of activity as the weeks went by, with games and matches becoming increasingly absurd. Each session would end up with a contest between the Roebucks and the Barclays where it always became our fervent ambition to manipulate the game and manufacture a 'glorious tie'. We rarely failed, and the children never seemed to notice. Whether we did Australian cricket much good I don't know, but our young pupils loved it and so did we in an exhausted sort of way. Mary-Lou did the organising, the two of us did the coaching and Tony Grieg came to watch his son, Mark, play. It was a happy event. Earlier I mentioned Peter as a potential politician; in fact he would also have made a very good teacher. He communicated well with the young, possibly less fluently with parents, particularly the mums. He didn't find women easy (he's not alone), and I got the feeling sometimes that he couldn't really see the point of them.

Our first really serious encounter on the field came in the 1978 Gillette Cup final in which Somerset were well fancied to beat Sussex. It was the might of Richards, Garner and Botham against Imran Khan and Javed Miandad. In the event it wasn't so much the great stars who took centre stage but the more humble county plodders. Chasing a score of 208 to win, I was going rather well until I fell into Botham's trap and tried to hook a short ball. Instead of it travelling gloriously and with speed to the square-leg boundary I merely ballooned the ball high up into the air where Roebuck took a good catch running round from mid-on.

Although Peter did not score many runs in that match, he was fast on his way to becoming a very effective player. He was a solid competitor, gritty, hard to get out and with an inclination to hit the ball through the legside, perhaps a spin-off from Viv Richards. As his career developed he became a heavy run-scorer and much respected by his peers in county cricket. He wasn't quite as much of a blocker as I was, but he would bat with a curious mixture of attack and discretion. Kenny Barrington and Chris Tavaré come to mind when I think of Roebuck. Both were more talented players who in their early years batted with much dash and flamboyance, but then retracted somewhat into their shells, inhibited perhaps by the pressures of playing for England. Roebuck never achieved that honour although he must have come jolly close to it at times. But he continued to score heavily for Somerset, particularly in his first two years as captain when he averaged almost 50 despite the internal strife and turmoil that had struck the club in the aftermath of the Richards, Garner and Botham era.

Without doubt Roebuck was brave, as much in the way he played and in his captaincy. He applied his brain to both and surprised many when he finally took on the leadership of Somerset and communicated his ideas to the team with both humility and simplicity. Of course, he didn't have the great team of the late seventies and early eighties at his disposal, but he made the best use he could of his own new side, bolstered up, if I remember, by the great talent of Martin Crowe and, later on, a young Steve Waugh.

The tussle over terminating Richards' and Garner's contracts, which culminated in an ugly row at an Extraordinary Meeting of members at the Shepton Mallet showground, wasn't for the faint-hearted. Emotions ran very high, as well they might as a glorious era in Somerset's cricket drew to a close. In the end the Somerset membership did realise that the club had to move on, and for that many were grateful for Roebuck's overall leadership. Few would have wanted to get involved in such a fracas, but Peter can at times be both single-minded and stubborn. Courting friendships has never been his scene, but he was always passionate about following his instincts and trying to do the right thing.

His clarity of thinking was a huge help to him, and his supporters, over the Shepton Mallet troubles. I imagine that brains come with advantages and disadvantages. Normal human beings expect quite a lot from the clever ones, believing they can work the oracle and hanging on their every word. And Peter did indeed exude a certain aura – he looked clever – and people tended therefore to believe in him. On one occasion he came in to bat at Taunton wearing only one side-piece to his batting helmet, leaving his right ear unprotected. Many of the Sussex players were intrigued by this new initiative, presumably taken to help improve his technique and there was even a move from one or two of them to emulate this unusual procedure. In due course, however, it transpired that Roebuck had merely lost the side-piece amidst the muddle at the bottom of his cricket case.

Then there was the unusual occasion at Worcester when Somerset exploited an obscure loophole in the Benson and Hedges competition rules and declared their innings closed at 1 for 0. "It must be Roebuck," came the shout from the Sussex dressing room, even though he was not captain at the time. Players were following the brain, not the logic. This sort of thing would never have been Roebuck's style, not even as a joke. He could be a difficult so-and-so at times but would never resort to 'pulling a fast one'. He's a most honest fellow, too much so at times, diplomacy never his strongest suit.

Occasionally he would do something stupid, which I found encouraging. He got out at Hove on one occasion; it may have been a poor decision or a bad shot or even a stupid run-out, but something had ruffled his feathers in the heat of the moment. As he returned to the pavilion he tapped the white railings quite firmly with his bat (as indeed I had done a few years earlier in a fit of pique) whereupon the entire structure collapsed in a heap, startling and indeed awakening some of our members.

Peter does have an angry streak in him; had he been a playwright, which he might well have been, I think he would have rivalled the likes of John Osborne and joined the ranks of angry young men. Whatever else Peter, whilst not giving time to social niceties, was never dull and even now will be stirring up emotions in Sydney as they absorb his prose over breakfast in the morning.

There is little doubt that Peter loves the game, maybe a bit of a love/hate relationship at times. Why else would he have been involved for so long? Indeed, after he had relinquished the captaincy of Somerset and handed over to Vic Marks, he was quickly and willingly absorbed by the next challenge – Minor Counties cricket and the leadership of Devon. I think he loved being the father figure, looked up to by the players, bowling a bit as well as batting and, above all, bringing on the young and encouraging them to enjoy the game. The teacher's instinct was ever-present in Peter's character.

So, Peter Roebuck, an unusual chap, self-contained and not everyone's cup of tea, but he was true to himself, and fiercely honest. He didn't seem to need many friends, but those he had were loyal and strong ones. Although he is a journalist now, based in Sydney, he is rather surprisingly living part of the time in Pietermaritsburg in Natal. I haven't quite worked that out but, let's be honest, Peter is quite hard to work out, a mysterious man whom I remember best as a young teacher living in a room at Cranbrook School, Sydney – untidy, clothes everywhere, smelly (not much washing went on) – immersed in a book, Molière or Voltaire possibly. Apart from books he didn't really go in for the finer things of life – although wine and food were exceptions – or deodorant, for that matter, for which he never had much time.

Robert Charles ('Jack') Russell

Born: Stroud, Gloucestershire, 15 August 1963

54 Tests for England (1988-1998)

1,897 runs at an average of 27.10, 2 centuries

153 catches and 12 stumpings

465 first-class matches (1981-2004)

16,861 runs at an average of 30.93, 11 centuries

1,192 catches and 128 stumpings

For some years Jack Russell was the outstanding wicket-keeper in English cricket. A distinctive figure in his floppy white hat, he was at his best when standing up to the wicket, his sure hands and quick reflexes able to handle even medium-pace bowling. His keeping was a key factor in Gloucestershire's winning of five one-day trophies in two years, in 1999 and 2000.

As a left-handed batsman with a style of his own, he was good enough to score two Test centuries, one against Australia, though his batting will be remembered best for the marathon, match-saving 29 not out that he scored in Johannesburg in November 1995. It was in the same match that he set a new Test record by taking 11 catches.

He played for Gloucestershire at the age of 17, postponing his Metalwork 'A' level exam and taking eight catches, a world record for a debutant, and he played for the last time at the age of 40. By then he was in sixth place in the all-time list of glovemen with 1,320 first-class dismissals. Add in his 565 in one-day games, and in all cricket only two keepers, Bob Taylor and Steve Rhodes, have claimed more victims.

A talented artist, he has a gallery in Chipping Sodbury.

Jack Russell

Jack is widely regarded as eccentric, a word that has been used not infrequently in my connection as well, but perception in this matter can be fickle. For sure he does have some strange ways, particularly where his diet is concerned, but he also has much depth to his personality and solid instincts too. To be fooled by a diet of Heinz baked beans and endless cups of tea would be too simplistic. Jack is, in fact, a man of rare insight and with a brain that confounds those who would dismiss him as 'Mad Jack'.

We toured South Africa together in 1995. Before then I only knew Jack from a distance, but on cricket tours you really find out about people. I was the Assistant Manager, responsible for the administration and organisation of the tour, so I got to know all the players very well – and in Jack I recognised something of a kindred spirit. After all, we were both a little odd but with the clarity of mind to know more or less what the form was.

In his funny way Jack is just about the most professional person I have ever met. Much of this he inherited from his mentor and friend Alan Knott, who was arguably England's best ever wicket-keeper-batsman. Knott was a loveable but strange fellow who dedicated his professional cricketing life to the pursuit of excellence, to the exclusion of just about anything else. Jack could not possibly have chosen a more impressive and brilliant example.

He had his own distinctive style as a wicket-keeper. He was neat, lithe and fluent in his movements, pleasing to the eye. In his stance he liked to incline his body towards mid-off, presumably to give him wider range outside the right-hander's off stump and to enable the slips to stand wider and cover more ground. Whether this affected his mobility down the leg-side I don't recall, but I never remember it being a problem. Although not as demanding as captaincy, the wicket-keeper is in effect the assistant director of the team, involved as he is in the action all the time. He sets the tone and tempo and at times has to hold the whole show together, particularly in periods of stress and anxiety. Jack played his part well and served the needs of his captain astutely and with flair. Just what was wanted.

His austere regime of self-discipline was demonstrated in his game. In his own way he coped well with pressure and was never 'flaky' when the going got tough – no excuses ever, just down-to-earth grit. I don't profess to be any sort of prophet, but I wrote in my diary early into the South African tour during a match at East London: "I believe Jack Russell will play a key role here; he has both confidence and outstanding commitment." A week or so later at Kimberley, where England played South Africa 'A', I went further: "Russell shows just the right balance between application and enterprise. He bats as though his life depends upon his performance." In short he looked on top of his game and in control. This was the match in which Paul Adams, with his extraordinary bowling action, first appeared on the scene to torment us. We were completely bewildered by this young fellow who in his delivery stride actually looked behind him and not at the batsman. England lost the game, and Adams took nine wickets in the match and grabbed the psychological high ground for the series.

Jack is a great patriot. He was enormously proud to be representing his country abroad in South Africa and, just before the start of the first Test match in Pretoria, he thrust a cassette into my hand and asked for its contents to be played on the loud-speaker system around the ground. About ten minutes before the start of play and to the slight surprise of the crowd, Elgar's *Pomp and Circumstance March No. 1* was followed by the *National Anthem*. Both blared out across Centurion Park. It was quite a concert. Jack stood to attention while Atherton and Stewart were busy strapping on their pads, concentrating on the matter in hand. This unilateral playing of anthems caused a bit of a stir and sent Ali Bacher, Managing Director of South African cricket, into a bit of a twitch. It was, I could see, awkward to have one national anthem played without the other. Questions would be asked and probably were. All were agreed that music, in this case the anthems, would get the matches off to a good start. This was easy enough for England but, so far as I can remember, South Africa in 1995 were still undecided about how to satisfy both new and old regimes. In the end a sort of medley was decided upon, which incorporated both the beautiful melody and atmosphere of *Nkosi Sikelele Afrika* and the original Nationalist march, *Die Stem*. From this point onwards national anthems became part of the first day's itinerary at Test matches, and both teams proudly lined up in front of the pavilion and sang the anthems with gusto. Jack had left his mark upon the matches before they even began.

There was much rain on the Highveld that November and it sadly stamped its soggy impression upon the match, but not before Jack, supporting a brilliant century by Graeme Hick, had raised the tempo of the game with a sprightly half-century. With thunder and lightning crashing and booming around him, the umpires had to drag him from the crease to the safety of the pavilion. And that was that; the ground was awash for the next three days. Jack was full of hope that the match would resume at some stage and looked longingly out at the rain-swept ground. By way of compensation we played chess together on the balcony just under cover from the wet. I rather fancied my chances after some bruising battles with Atherton which I thought had warmed me up nicely. I had three matches with Jack and lost the lot. He's a crafty little tactician and with a keen brain.

The relationship between players and managers is a very important one. Trust and respect are two of the most important ingredients, and they should be mutually strong. Although a tour of South Africa is just about as good as it gets, it's still a long tour and with a considerable preamble before the Test matches begin. Form can be an elusive beast, and inevitably players miss home too. So I always left my room door open for anyone who wanted to pop in for a drink or a cup of tea in the evening. I had frequent visitors of whom Jack was one of the regulars. Always a cup of tea it was for him with the bag dipped delicately into the hot water twice before being discarded. Very strange. The team room, or my room as it turned out, became a source of strength both for me and for those who came along to visit it.

Mercifully there was no time for chess during the second Test match played at the Wanderers in Johannesburg. From the moment we won the toss and elected to field, we were up against it. The only positive and exciting thing to happen during the first three days was that Jack broke the world record for catches – eleven – a feat which by no means put England into a winning position.

It is the last day that I remember mostly. England had to bat all day to save the game, having already lost four wickets overnight. Atherton and Robin Smith began the fight back; Russell was next man in.

My day began strangely. My task was to drive out to the airport where I had to greet Aileen Russell who, unbeknownst to her husband Jack, was making a surprise visit to Johannesburg. The reason for this was that she had never been on a tour before, permission not given by Jack, who didn't want anything to distract him. I eventually identified Aileen in the arrivals hall whence I whisked her back to the Sandton Sun Hotel where she was ushered up to Jack's room to await his arrival later and surprise him.

The outcome of the match at the Wanderers is now well known to everyone. Atherton batted for twelve hours or more and Russell over four hours for his 29. By any standards this was an heroic partnership, and it saved the day. During the unfolding drama I sat inside the quaint, old-fashioned and charming pavilion. It was not a happy place to be while Atherton and Russell got under the skin of South Africa. Cork, as next man in, was pacing up and down in a state of nervous jitters, making constant and understandable visits to the loo. Gough, Fraser and Malcolm were also preparing for batting just in case. I felt I was trapped in the inner sanctum of hell, but it would have been cowardly to leave. Out on the balcony were the others who were bravely tormenting themselves by watching the game as it reached its climax. Possibly this was Atherton's and Russell's greatest match; a celebration drink at the end would, I think, have been quite in order. But somehow I had to divert Jack from such temptations so I sat him on the wall outside the hotel while he did interview after interview before I suggested he should return to his room. To be fair, Jack did not look at his best – unshaven, cap on head, dirty clothes from the day's play clinging to him like seaweed and smelly – he needed a shower. So up he went, room key at the ready and opened the door to meet his fate.

Jack was not a dapper dresser but he was very particular about his clothing. His equipment was often stuck together with tape, and he was a dab hand with needle and thread. His most sacred possession was his hat, an ungainly and unfashionable white floppy affair, and deeply loved as an essential part of his wicket-keeping equipment. Alan Knott, his mentor, had worn a similar old hat so Jack may have thought this was the secret of success – who knows? The cricketing world in general was faintly amused by Jack's hat. It was after all his trademark. The hat was eccentric but appeared to pose no threat to anyone; it was simply a vital part of Jack's psychological armour.

All was well until Ali Bacher saw him and took a dislike to the hat. The problem was that the hat was white and did not match the sponsored blue kit being worn by the England players in one-day internationals. Oh dear, something would have to give. Would Bacher and the sponsors be able to cope with this crisis? Well, they did and came up with a clever solution which kept all parties reasonably happy. Solomon himself could have done no better. Jack, using his needle and thread, sowed a blue hat onto the shabby white one, creating a two-tiered hat. A new fashion. Jack was pleased that his own precious hat was still snugly placed on his head while Bacher and the sponsors could proudly watch the blue hat in action, matching the outfit and clearly showing up on television. Thus was the outcome of Jack's hat crisis unexpectedly satisfactory.

Perhaps Jack's greatest asset as a cricketer, giving him the ability to cope with peaks and troughs, was his skill as a painter. On a day off, his easel, paints and brushes were never far from his side. This was his way of escaping, or switching off, in just the same way as I would go fishing. The bonus was that Jack was as talented with his oils as he was with bat and wicket-keeping gloves. It did not take long for him to become as renowned for his paintings, landscapes mainly, as he was for his cricket. His work is now sold all over the world.

In South Africa he took two days off after the third Test match in Durban to visit Rorke's Drift in Natal and capture the atmosphere of Zulu warfare in the late 19th century. Jack was fascinated by the grim struggle that ensued at Rorke's Drift and *Zulu* the film was a constant comfort to him on tour, with Michael Caine and Stanley Baker his close companions.

*

The following winter England visited Zimbabwe and New Zealand, and I was now the tour manager. The selected party was a strange mix of people, chosen, I think, more for their individual qualities than for their collective merit as a team. Few of the party really knew where they stood, and differing values had an unsettling effect upon the overall sense of purpose. The chemistry which underlies team members and attitudes is enormously important to the effectiveness of any mission, particularly overseas, and it took a long while for the squad to settle. Indeed, it wasn't until we reached New Zealand, with the pressure off a little, that performances began to reflect the potential of the side.

Jack found himself out on a limb and, despite his strength of resolve and spirit, was omitted from most of the matches. Alec Stewart took on the dual role of batsman and wicket-keeper, which was understandable, but for me it had always been a comfort to see Jack walking to the crease at number seven. He never appeared to grumble about his plight which, I suppose, made him easier to drop. But despite this blow he was always first on the coach each morning, with his cap perched on his head and ready for action.

I think Jack took the view that, if he couldn't play cricket, he would fulfil his purpose in life by painting. The Zimbabwean and New Zealand scenery became a paradise for him, a sort of unexpected painting holiday. He hardly played in New Zealand, indeed he may not have played at all, and he took himself up into the hills and painted some landscapes for which his talent was so well suited and which took his mind away from his primary profession.

Jack played his cricket like a feather-weight boxer. He fought tenaciously all the time, jabbing away and gradually grinding down his opponents by the intense pressure he exerted. His 124 against India at Lord's in 1996 and his 29 not out against South Africa in Johannesburg were both outstanding innings. There were many others, too. In the school of Alan Knott his professional attention to detail marked him out as one of the country's most effective wicket-keepers since the war. In addition he had a sharp cricket brain which he put to good use on the field and in the dressing room. Russell's name on the team sheet was as reassuring to England as it was unsettling for the opposition. His record is testament to that.

Timothy Miles Bindon Rice

Born: Amersham, Buckinghamshire, 10 November 1944

Tim Rice is a lyricist whose collaborations with the composer Andrew Lloyd Webber created the musicals Joseph and the Amazing Technicolor Dreamcoat, Jesus Christ Superstar *and* Evita. *He has worked with other composers on* Chess, Heathcliff *and* The Lion King.

With his brother Jonathan and disc jockeys Mike Read and Paul Gambaccini he created the Guinness Book of Hit Singles, *which he edited for twenty years from 1977.*

In July 1973 he organised a group of friends to play a cricket match at Bicester, and so much did he enjoy the day that the team turned into the Heartaches Cricket Club, a wandering side which he still captains 600 games and 40 years on and for which he produces a yearly handbook full of detailed match reports and copious statistics. His own batting average falls some way short of double figures, but the team remains in good health, winning as many matches as it loses.

He served as President of MCC in 2002.

Tim Rice

Leicester Forest Service Station, sitting astride the M1, will not strike many as a place of unconfined creativity. Indeed, it was not for that reason that I turned off the motorway. I was tired after a lot of driving, in need of a rest and a cup of coffee to liven me up.

I sat for a while on my own at a table overlooking the surging traffic of the evening rush hour. Music was blaring from the internal system and, alongside, a carpenter banged nails into a piece of wood by the Kentucky Fried Chicken stall. The air was polluted by noise and dust. It was not peaceful. And yet I felt strangely at home in that unpleasant environment. No one was pestering me.

Sipping my coffee and recovering as I did so, my thoughts turned to Tim Rice. I had been invited to write about him for a book which Christopher Bazalgette of the Hampshire Hogs was compiling, an unusual memoir in which most of the text consisted of people other than Christopher writing about yet other people. In my case, for some reason which escapes me, I was having to write about Tim Rice.

What did I know of Tim? He is a great cricket lover and has been on the MCC committee with me. He is also a trustee of the Arundel Castle Cricket Foundation. But first and foremost he has been a most successful lyricist. So, sitting in the service station, I found myself wondering whether any of his great works had been completed in such an unpromising atmosphere. Could genius possibly find expression amidst the traffic's roar and the relentlessly blaring music? Probably not and yet, by the same token, Tim is an unusual chap. I felt it not impossible that one of his masterpieces could have emanated from such uninspring circumstances.

I don't know about you, but I have never been sure how great lyricists and musicians put words and music together without falling out with each other. What comes first? The words or the music? Perhaps it's a mixture of the two. The trick, I imagine, must be in the partnership, the meeting of minds, the empathy of purpose. Maybe that's the answer.

It was only quite late in life that I came to realise that lyrics really are quite important and how they do need to fit the tune. For ages I thought only the melody mattered. That must have been before *Joseph* first appeared on stage. All of a sudden we had a strong story – a familiar one from the Old Testament – music that was jolly and tuneful, accompanied by witty and descriptive words. I took the family to see it at the Palladium some years ago when the highlight was Jason Donovan, as Joseph, soaring high above the audience on a precarious device. This added to the excitement of the show and was particularly appreciated by my daughter, Georgina, whose early years had been dominated by episodes of *Neighbours*.

There is little doubt that Tim, notwithstanding his cricketing prowess and great love of the game, knows more about pop and popular music and, for all I know, every other type of music, than most people living. He knows the people and the culture and is an encyclopaedia when it comes to names, dates and songs.

What Tim does have, which a lot don't, is loads of wit and charm. He's fun. Apart from that he is very tall, probably the first thing you'll notice about him and then, next, he has the most marvellous voice which must have kept him out of trouble right from the beginning. His voice, knowledge and charm must have opened the door to broadcasting and game shows, of which my favourite is *Just a Minute* with Nicholas Parsons. Although quite competitive, I suspect Tim has never actually won the show, although he just may have done once on a very good day and with the help of the other contestants. I suppose Tim would have made a very capable game show host, *Strictly Come Dancing* or that sort of thing. But in truth I think he's a bit above all that. He does have a touch of class, although not so much as a batsman or bowler.

So there I was, still at the service station, writing my piece. It was rather thrilling to write a few words about a famous person, more so than you may imagine, aware as I am of how turbulent and precarious it must be to climb up the greasy pole. There must have been hours spent listening to pop songs, many a B-side to fend off and out-and-out stinkers to cast aside. And yet the product of all this has been words and ideas set to music, giving us rhythm, metre and much wit; a touch of genius in fact for which the world is most grateful. I imagine that

Tim's life is rich with words and melody which have helped to shape our culture and perhaps even burrowed into our psyche.

Apart from music, Tim loves cricket. The two have been close companions in the past. For many years Neville Cardus wrote about music and cricket in the *Manchester Guardian* and captured the atmosphere of both pursuits with prose that has scarcely been equalled since. Tim always claims with modesty that in the cricketing department both skill and co-ordination passed him by when talent was shared out. I suspect he was a bit better than that but have yet to see evidence to suggest so. Possibly he was a fair player in his younger days, a dark horse, hidden talents lurking up his sleeve. But I doubt it. I prefer to think that he wasn't much good and indeed quite proud of his slender ability. Lack of ability does at least give others a chance to shine.

In the end, little though I knew about Tim and his work as a lyricist, I found a way of putting my thoughts into five pages of writing. I read it back, and some of it didn't seem too bad. So I tucked it into my briefcase and continued my journey to speak at an evening do in Nottingham.

The next day I drove south to Oxford to have lunch with my son who was at university there. Despite being in his final year, he was full of beans when I greeted him at his college and suggested we make our way to the Head of the River pub alongside the Thames by Folly Bridge. He was clutching under his arm the latest draft of his thesis and I my few words on Tim Rice. We were planning to read to each other over lunch. It was a cold day, but the sun was shining.

We sat outside and ordered drinks and food – a burger for him and seafood platter for me, accompanied by tartare sauce in a pot. I secured my handwritten Tim Rice prose to the table by planting the tartare sauce on top and waited for lunch to arrive which in due course it did. For a while all was calm until, unthinkingly, I lifted up the pot of tartare sauce with the intention of putting some on my plate. It was a foolish thing to do. In just a whisker, disaster struck. The mild breeze wafted my pages up into the air whereupon they fluttered about, suspended above the river before alighting gently upon the cold water.

I shouted in panic as Tim Rice began to sink. But there was still hope. The force of the Thames flowing downstream had created a strong back-eddy or current. There was just a chance that my precious pages might float round and back to us before submerging. Amidst the mayhem Theo, my son, got hold of a long punt pole and began swishing it about by way of a rescue operation. With great dexterity he retrieved two of the five pages as they floated round. The remaining three pages sadly sank, overcome by the treacherous current. In time they would float downstream, bound for the docks unless intercepted by a hungry fish on the way. We laid the two rescued pages, with the ink running, on chairs to dry in the sun.

Some three hundred years ago George Frederick Handel lost some of his music for the Royal Fireworks celebration when a spark got into the papers and set light to part of the score. By comparison, my disaster was only a very minor setback.

Back in the quiet of my home I attempted a re-write. But instead of fresh inspiration I found I was simply trying to remember what I had written the first time. It didn't quite work so I finished up telling the story of how the pages had blown into the Thames. It was not, as it turned out, what Christopher Bazalgette's editor wanted, and a much abridged entry appeared in the book.

Whether my original piece, born amid the infernal blare of Leicester Forest Service Station, displayed some well-expressed insight into Tim Rice, I'm not sure. But I did enjoy writing it.

John Michael Brearley

Born: Harrow, Middlesex, 28 April 1942

39 Tests for England (1976-1981)

1,442 runs at an average of 22.88

31 Tests as captain

455 first-class matches (1961-1983)

25,186 runs at an average of 37.81, 45 centuries

418 catches and 12 stumpings

Mike Brearley was one of the great England captains, combining rare tactical insight with an outstanding ability to get the best out of the individuals in his teams.

In the summer of 1964, playing for Cambridge University and Middlesex, he was a good enough batsman to score 2,178 runs, a total bettered only by Tom Graveney and Eric Russell. This led to his selection for the tour of South Africa that winter, though he did not play in the Tests.

For several years his cricket took second place in his life, as he forged an academic career as a lecturer in Philosophy at the University of Newcastle, but he came back to the game full-time in 1971 when he was offered the captaincy of Middlesex. Rebuilding the team, he led them to four Championship titles between 1976 and 1982.

In 1975 he was, with Boycott, one of only two English batsmen to average 50 in the season, and in 1976 he finally made his Test debut. With Tony Greig's defection to World Series Cricket the following year he assumed the captaincy. He won Ashes series in 1977, in 1978/79 and most famously, when recalled in mid-series, in 1981.

He left cricket to pursue a career in psychoanalysis. In 2008, just after his year as President of MCC, he became President of the British Psychoanalytical Society.

Mike Brearley

"John, don't you want to know the truth?"

I was having lunch in the President's box at Lord's during the Test match in 2011, between England and India, and was sitting opposite Mike Brearley when he flicked this provocative and profound question across the table to me. It clearly required an answer.

The 'truth' in question came from a simple, standard, run-of-the-mill cricket appeal. The Indians were shouting for a catch to the wicket-keeper off Kevin Pietersen. The umpire, Billy Bowden, raised his crooked finger, and that appeared to be that. A judgement, which used to be final, had been made. But no; Pietersen thought otherwise, as well he might, and sent a sign to the third umpire pleading for mercy. After a short delay he was reprieved. Technology had decreed there was no edge, and Bowden presumably felt embarrassed.

The 'truth', though, represented the challenge. I knew that a complicated discussion with Brearley, with both psychology and technology at the forefront, would be a mistake; I would certainly not come out on top. My arguments were frail, too – little confidence in 'hot-spot' where I thought only howlers were supposed to warrant a reversed decision. But enough of that. 'Truth' is all very well so long as it's compatible with respect, trust and common sense, as well as with the latest technology.

The good thing about Brearley is that he doesn't go in for arguments, let alone rows, but he's always game for a discussion. Without doubt there is a certain aura about the man; he speaks quite slowly with clear diction, rarely uses long words and never talks down to people. Astonishingly he has never made me feel stupid, and I think the same would apply to others. He is blessed with a clear mind and a good brain, stored it would seem within a large head now sporting white hair which gives him a bit more the air of a professor but not, I think, a mad one. It is his clarity of thinking which I have always found impressive, the ability to sort out a seemingly complicated and muddled situation in a way that is perfectly clear to all. "How come I didn't think it out like that?" I'd find myself saying, along with many others.

There is no doubt that Brearley is what you might call a 'clever chap'. A good memory, logical thinking, excellent with people. Tactically ahead of the game – and, above all else, a good listener. He has to be. He has built and shaped his career as a psychoanalyst by listening and only responding when he has something helpful to say. His great cricketing work, *The Art of Captaincy*, used now as an important reference to many courses and seminars on leadership, could just as well have been called *The Art of Listening* – though it might not have sold so many copies. Brearley is not one to blurt out an answer; he will listen and think before producing a measured response.

It is a feather in the cap for cricket that Brearley chose to devote so much of his time to it. As an undergraduate student at Cambridge in the early sixties he excelled both on the cricket field and academically. He has, of course, been richly acclaimed for his captaincy and leadership skills, but it should not be forgotten that in the early days he was a rising star with the bat, both at Cambridge and with Middlesex. Indeed, in 1964 he scored over 2,000 runs and was, as a result, selected to tour South Africa with Mike Smith's successful campaign in 1964/65. On that trip he played a supporting role, making useful runs in the provincial games but failing to play in a Test match. Without doubt, though, his attitude and philosophy towards South African politics, and apartheid in particular, must have been taking shape as the tour developed. His fertile mind began to grapple with its implications.

Immediately after leaving Cambridge, and despite the minor success on tour in South Africa, Brearley's prominence in the cricket world appeared to wane a little as academic priorities kicked in more strongly. It wasn't until 1967 on a tour with MCC Under-25 that he hit the headlines again by scoring 312 not out in Pakistan's North-West frontier city of Peshawar and reminding the world that he was more than just a great thinker in the making. A week or two later in Dacca, then in East Pakistan, now Bangladesh, he scored 223 and shared in a partnership of 356 with Dennis

Amiss. It is tempting to suggest that, had Brearley applied himself more to his cricket in his early to mid-twenties, his career record as a Test match batsman might have been considerably enhanced. Something had to give, though, amidst this overload of talent and, in the end, it was probably his Test match average. But, as Brearley was to discover in due course, there was a lot more to life than that.

During the mid to late 1960s Brearley took what might now be called a self-imposed sabbatical from top-class cricket. His intellect was successfully employed elsewhere, and it gave him time to pursue interests that were close to his heart. One of these was the troublesome business of England's relationship with South Africa which had been fraught with problems before and after its refusal to admit England batsman Basil D'Oliveira to the country because the colour of his skin did not suit the South African government's racial policies.

Brearley felt very strongly that MCC should have no association with a South African Cricket Board that was supported by a government committed to a policy of apartheid. He joined forces with former England captain David Sheppard, the Bishop of Woolwich and long-time social activist, to become founder members of the 'Fair Cricket Campaign'. This group was established to protest against the proposed tour of South Africa to England in 1970. Following the D'Oliveira affair and in the context of widespread international outrage with the South African government, an important and more militant minority felt that supporting a tour with an all-white South African team was morally wrong. Many of them formed part of the 'Stop the Seventy Tour Campaign' – a group of Young Liberals led by future Labour Cabinet Minister, Peter Hain, then only 19 years old. Hain and his supporters, despite sharing the same aim as Brearley and Sheppard, sought to achieve their objectives by the use of 'direct action'. Brearley, throughout, felt that it would be more beneficial to adopt a calmer, more measured approach, and certainly not a violent one. As a result he wrote several forthright letters to Billy Griffith, then secretary of MCC, and these were by no means the only ones Mr Griffith received. He was inundated with correspondence, from both supporters and critics of the tour.

Brearley realised, unlike many others, that this was not a dispute over the scheduling of a tour. In the context of world-wide protest, youth activism and the ever-present fear of communist infiltration, Hain's movement seemed to many to challenge not just apartheid but Britishness itself. Brearley sensibly and sensitively wanted to emphasise his views without spreading notions of fear which Hain and the 'Stop the Seventy Tour Campaign' sought to exploit. While it remains unclear which group had more influence, the tour was ultimately cancelled at the request of the British government a month or so before the South African players were due to arrive. Brearley emerged from the affair with his reputation substantially enhanced.

The breadth of Brearley's ambitions did not leave him with as much time for cricket as probably he would have wished. Yet, in 1971 at the age of 29, he took up the challenge of full-time first-class cricket again as captain of Middlesex. And it can't have been that easy to marshal a fine, talented but perhaps slightly cliquey and ageing group of players including Titmus and Parfitt, both of whom had already captained the club, as well as Murray, Price and Russell. All five had played for England and imposed their considerable influence upon the game. By 1976 only Titmus remained, and Middlesex were crowned county champions with a new crop of young players, over whom Brearley could exert his measured style to greater purpose.

Brearley's skill as a leader lay in the two-fold effect of his sensitive management of players from all backgrounds, cultural and economic, combined with his tactical good sense. He not only moved his men around as he might do in a game of chess, but he also understood their values and potential for success. In short he got the best out of his resources. Strangely enough there was nothing fancy about this; if anything was clever it was the simplicity of the plans which were easily interpreted by the players. Ray Illingworth's approach, which I also admire, was probably tougher and less compromising but no less effective for it. Brearley, though, did have the extraordinary ability to get on well with less educated professionals and understood how they ticked and all without a hint of condescension.

It has frequently been argued that Brearley's ability as a batsman fell short of international standard despite his success as a captain. Indeed, his record as an opener would suggest as much. But, make no mistake, Brearley was a very good county player who won his initial Test caps on the back of his first-class performances. I wouldn't say he was a total natural, but he made himself into a very good player – self-made, if you like. His batting in 1976 was rewarded with two Test caps against the West Indies (not easy for starters!) and won him the vice-captaincy under Tony Greig in India that winter. As captain, he later presided over three Ashes series victories in addition to success against Pakistan and New Zealand. The record is impressive, even if Australia were suffering from post-Packer syndrome at the time.

For all that, in the eyes of many Brearley was not perfect. For a start he was very much a Sixties man, endearingly scruffy and lacking any sort of clothes sense. He wasn't very much at home with the established view of things and abhorred any sort of pomp or show. Just like Mike Atherton some twenty years later, 'image', with its public relations responsibilities, was anathema to him. He hated it. At times too his sensitivity got the better of him which included the odd flash of temper which, if nothing else, showed he cared a lot.

I found it very encouraging to watch from the balcony at Lord's and see Brearley lose his cool during a Benson and Hedges quarter-final match between Middlesex and Sussex. It had been a bad-tempered affair throughout, caused largely by the understandably aggressive nature of Imran Khan and Daniel's fast bowling. Jackie van Geloven, the umpire, became flustered, and things appeared to get out of hand with Brearley and Imran on the cusp of grappling with each other late in the Sussex innings. Things were made even worse by the uncalled-for intervention of a young Gatting who rushed like a footballer from the deep to rescue his captain from impending assault. The effect was immediate. Brearley who, up until then, was venting his wrath towards Imran, quickly turned his attention upon Gatting, the young pup, with whom he was furious. Brearley's face, even from the Lord's balcony, was enough to turn the milk sour in the dressing room. The long and short of it, and there was admittedly quite a lot of short, was a swift decline in Sussex's batting defence and a fairly rapid victory march for Middlesex.

Later in the same season, one of unremitting success for Middlesex, I captained a championship match between Sussex and Middlesex over the August Bank Holiday at Hove. I wasn't actually the Sussex captain at the time but acting in the role in place of Arnold Long, who was giving me the opportunity to gain some experience in the task. I tossed the coin with Brearley which came down in my favour. I felt at least I had won the first trick and elected to field, largely I fear as a cowardly device to avoid the fearsome Middlesex bowling attack of Daniel, Van der Bijl, Selvey, Emburey and Edmonds. By the end of the day Middlesex had scored 360 for four wickets. Brearley made 114 and everyone else made runs, too. I was reduced to bowling myself for much of the time – and indeed took three wickets – but this was mainly as an apology to the rest of the team who had to tolerate a long, hot and unnecessary day in the field. It was a bad day, at least it was for me. The captaincy issue for 1981 had yet to be decided. I had done myself no favours.

After the day's play I met up with Brearley for a drink and congratulated him upon his innings. I confessed that I felt a little crestfallen, and we agreed that my decision earlier in the day had not been a great success. But Brearley looked up at me while I sipped my drink and said a few words that I have always remembered. I am loath to quote anyone for fear of getting it wrong or missing the point, but the gist of Brearley's message was this: "Once you have made a decision, having assembled together all the evidence, the outcome is then largely out of your control." He had no reason to throw me a crumb of comfort but, as I drove home that night, I felt more at peace with the world than at any time during the day. It's hardly a surprise that Brearley has made such a success of his psychoanalysis practice.

Brearley was one of those captains who tended to do precisely what you didn't want him to do. His control over people was slightly hypnotic. There is little doubt in my mind that his ultimate achievement came from his leadership skills and that his ability to excel in this sphere was derived from his standing on no great high board of excellence himself. Thus he had the time to think of others and get the best out of them. I dare say he wrestled with this a bit because I suspect he would dearly have loved to excel more himself. He didn't lead from the front but rather from within his own circle of players and the mutual respect that emerged as a result.

I am sure I will be challenged on my final assertion. It seems to me that, not infrequently, strong leaders are poor judges of what is required to succeed them. Brearley, in retrospect, probably got it wrong when endorsing Ian Botham so strongly to lead England first against a powerful West Indies side and then Australia. I dare say he felt that a style entirely different from his own was appropriate for the team. Football clubs rarely get it right either, and in politics neither Thatcher nor Blair after long administrations were able to secure a satisfactory legacy. More often than not success does not breed success. In Brearley's case he was, of course, given a second chance and grabbed it in 1981 after the Lord's Test match when Botham fell on his sword amidst much publicity.

Doug Insole, Brearley's manager in Australia in the late seventies, chose him in 2006 to succeed him as President of MCC. It was a refreshing and enlightened decision as Brearley will never quite sit closely with the cricketing establishment. It is that, for me, that makes him so interesting and different from many others. But he is quietly confident, a good man in a crisis, composed and completely honest. He believes in the truth and challenges those who seek an alternative route.

Peter John Eaton

Born: Hastings, 26 July 1942
Died: Durham, 9 February 2000

Peter Eaton worked for 37 years as a groundsman at Hove: five years as assistant to Len Creese, then 32 years as Head Groundsman.

Three times he was named Groundsman of the Year.

Peter Eaton

Throughout my career Peter (fondly know as H.G. – Head Groundsman) was constantly and with some justification rude about my cricket. He would bark at me as I prodded his precious pitch at Hove. "What on earth are you doing that for?" he'd ask. "It's not green enough," came my reply, "not enough grass; you should see Trent Bridge." "Bollocks," he would mutter vehemently under his breath. Most days started something like this. I retold this story in the address I gave at his funeral in the crematorium chapel high up on the South Downs on a mizzly February day. I think the 'Bollocks' took the congregation and rector a bit by surprise, but it made H.G.'s family in the front row and many others rock with laughter.

Peter came from Hastings and was introduced to Hove by his mentor and father-figure of groundsmen, Len Creese, whom I remember as a fairly gruff character of the old school but who, for all that, knew how to grow grass and tend the pitch. Len was head groundsman at Hove for a short while in the late 1960s, during which he sold me my first full-size, short-handle, sub-standard cricket bat. With his dirty hands he smeared a little linseed oil onto the blade and explained that it was only sub-standard, because of a couple of small knots in the grain and therefore came a little cheaper. I was delighted and returned with it to school aged 16 where, as luck would have it, I scored a lot of runs, including my first century.

When Len left the County Ground and returned to home territory in Hastings he sent Peter over to Hove instead, probably aged then only 25 and surely by far the youngest groundsman to assume such prominent responsibility. It did not take him long to make his mark. "The worst bloody groundsman we've ever seen," we constantly told him. But we knew he wasn't. He started winning awards – groundsman of the year, that sort of thing – but these triumphs never came near to turning his head. He remained true to himself throughout – scruffy, grubby, an unwashed look about him, dirty hands and filthy fingernails – just right in fact.

Whether or not he scrubbed up a bit before he went to bed at night or still smelt faintly of engine oil I don't know, but he was someone to whom I think Lady Chatterley might have taken a fancy, had the opportunity arisen. Tallish and quite handsome too in a rough, chummy sort of way he was, and with a twinkle in his eye which some might have found quite alluring. Peter had the attributes that might just turn the head of an aristocrat in search of adventure. As it was he was devoted to his wife, Jacqui, his two boys, Mark and Barry, and Alsatians, Duke and Baron. They all lived together in a tiny and indescribably chaotic house by the ground and next to the pub. It was here that, amongst other things, they entertained many of the match umpires who, wishing to save on expenses, were prepared to put up with the discomfort and mild squalor. But the Eaton hospitality was so generous and genuine, coming as it did from the heart, that it ensured good marks for pitches in return for such a warm welcome.

One of my favourite umpires who often stayed with Peter in those days was Sam Cook, a compact, balding and strongly built Gloucestershire man who spoke just as you would expect him to with a throaty burr to his country voice – cigarettes the culprit to some extent. He became my greatest friend amongst the umpires. You see, in his day, he had been a slow bowler – a left-arm spinner who, in his early days, would have been much influenced by Tom Goddard. Later in the Gloucestershire team of the 1950s and '60s he complemented the off-spinning craft of John Mortimore and David Allen. I was impressed by all of that, but my main interest in Sam (C. Cook) was that he was a great supporter and fan of spin bowlers and took a liking to both my style of bowling (moderate off-spin) and me. I could tell he was on my side when he was umpiring, and so I always tried to bowl from his end which was never a problem once I became captain of Sussex. Then, not only did I find he was enthusiastic about my bowling but I also had the advantage of his knowing that at the end of the match I would be marking the umpire's card. I knew I was on to a good thing.

I really liked Sam, which was just as well because he didn't have many friends amongst the batsmen on the county circuit who feared his energetic index finger. He had a reputation as an 'outer' which didn't suit batsmen keen to make a name for themselves. Kepler Wessels, our brilliant South African and at some time Australian opening batsman, used to shudder and shake with anxiety and begin to twitch slightly (a bit like Herbert Lom in the *Pink Panther* films) when he saw Sam. Poor Kepler would curl up miserably on a sofa in his corner of the dressing-room and read his Bible in the hope that the Almighty might see off this impending threat to his average. He never quite came to terms with Sam.

Believe it or not, Sam was one of the few people I knew who really thought I could bowl, so he took to coaching me during the matches we shared together. "Make sure you get down my end," he'd whisper when we passed each other. "I'll see you're all right." Well, if this wasn't heaven, almost too good to be true, he would gently coach me during my bowling spells. "A little slower, I think," he would murmur between clenched teeth. "Try round the wicket and what about that swinger of yours?" I always did as I was told. Sam, you see, liked the game to move on – progress, he called it – and I knew that, if I could just hit the batsman on the pads, I was in with a chance. Sam was, without doubt, the most obliging umpire I knew and the friendliest, partly because he liked me but also because he had half an eye on an early finish which, with trains to catch or traffic to negotiate, was always central to his way of thinking. A match ending in two days was ideal and persistent rain the next best thing.

There was a meeting at Lord's each year involving all the county captains who offered opinions upon the standard of umpiring. Bob Willis, representing Warwickshire and England, was adamant that there should be an agreed minimum standard. "No worse than Sam Cook," he stated firmly.

In those days the umpires changed at Hove in a tiny room next to the groundsman's dugout. The dugout itself took the form of an underground cellar, crypt-like, beneath the Committee Room of the main pavilion. It was more like a squatter's den than a groundsman's hut – a mess, a lovely mess. Tools and machinery were scattered about willy-nilly; cigarette ends, oil, cans of half-drunk beer and girlie magazines were strewn over the concrete floor. Players would be constant visitors seeking consolation and sanctuary after getting out. "Bloody silly shot," was about all the consolation they got, but they still turned up for H.G. to add salt to the wound. Ian Gould would nip down there to chat up the umpires and snitch a fag or two. There would be times in a match when the dugout was the centre of social activity, particularly on a bad day.

Groundsmen and their impact upon the game have always been undervalued. Without sound pitches which offer something for bat and ball good cricket is hard to play, and for years H.G. produced marvellous surfaces – greenish at times for sure but with good grass and the pace that comes in its wake. The ball came firmly onto the bat, moved about a bit off the seam and carried to the wicket-keeper and slips. Uncontrived results were possible in three days. Just occasionally the ball would spin but, if not, at least it bounced a bit. A good spinner might have his chance to get into the game, but I took very few wickets at Hove.

On the whole it was the fast bowlers who were inspired by these conditions. Wayne Daniel roared down the hill on more than one occasion and bowled with fearsome speed, causing injury to both body and pride. Viv Richards had his day too, batting on those fast pitches forcing a ball, I well remember, from John Snow off the back foot high over mid-on and on to the top of the Gilligan stand to the south side of the ground. H.G.'s pitches gave both bowlers and batsman an equal chance to flourish; this remarkable talent made an enormous contribution to our matches.

For thirty years or more H.G. was consistently at or near the top of the leader board, and in true Sussex tradition this was very much a family affair in which the Eatons ruled the roost at Hove as caretakers of a ground they loved and in an era when the groundsman was less highly valued than should have been the case.

David Lloyd

Born: Accrington, Lancashire, 18 March 1947

9 Tests for England (1974-1975)
552 runs at an average of 42.46, 1 century
407 first-class matches (1965-1983)
19,269 runs at an average of 33.33, 38 centuries
237 wickets at an average of 30.26

David Lloyd was an attractive left-handed batsman in the Lancashire side which won six one-day trophies between 1969 and 1975, the Red Rose county's only sustained spell of success since the early 1930s.

He was selected to open the innings for England against India in 1974, taking the place of Geoff Boycott, and in his second match, at Edgbaston, he hit an unbeaten 214, the highest score of his career. Later in the summer, against Pakistan, he hit a one-day hundred, but his England career was brought to an end that winter when he came up against the unnerving pace of Australia's Lillee and Thomson.

He captained Lancashire for five years, then after cricket had a spell as an umpire before becoming Lancashire's coach. His fresh ideas and infectious enthusiasm led to his appointment in 1996 as England coach, a post he held for three years.

He is now a hugely successful after-dinner speaker and television commentator, mixing humour, a deep knowledge of the game and an idiosyncratic turn of phrase, made all the more popular by his strong Accrington accent.

In 2009, his love of the game undimmed, he was still playing cricket – for Accrington, alongside his son Graham. On the last afternoon, at the age of 62, he struck the winning runs that won the club the Lancashire League.

David Lloyd

David did not like Zimbabwe nor did he like Zimbabweans. That was quite plain. On an Under-19 tour early in 1996 they rubbed each other up the wrong way and nothing, from that point onwards, was likely to bring about a truce. Admittedly Harare was a hot and intimidating city, set in the centre of the country, claustrophobic in many ways and without the advantage of a sea breeze to fan the atmosphere. Mugabe's oppressive regime hardly lightened the feel of a country treading on egg-shells.

Lloyd succeeded Illingworth as England's head coach in April 1996 and got his eye in with home series against India and Pakistan. He was what you might call the new style of modern coach – a lot of action, energy and enthusiasm, mixed with boundless chat in an endearing Accrington accent. He was quite different from what had gone before. Jaunty and bouncy he was and with a brain overflowing with new ideas and drills for practice, as well as challenging suggestions for the players.

His style was exhausting, but he was tireless in his efforts to achieve good things and results for England. This was why Atherton chose him, someone to put a bit of pep into proceedings despite coming with something of a 'handle with care' sticker on the package. Lloyd, according to Atherton, could become emotional and quite stirred up in moments of drama and tension. Indeed, I'm reliably told that the Lancashire players would try to lock him away in the coach's room as matches came to the boil. But Lloyd really did care and wore his heart on his sleeve. He was very bright and quick-witted, if a little wild.

In his earlier days he was full of beans as a player, brave and always up for the battle. He would stride briskly in to open the batting for Lancashire with his partner, Barry Wood, and say a polite "Good morning" to everyone as if he were attending a meeting in the office. But, no mistake, he was very serious about his cricket and although he never mastered Geoff Arnold's bowling – he had a thing about him – he conquered the Indian spinners – Venkataraghavan, Prasanna and Bedi – at Edgbaston in 1974 where he scored 214 for England. His success during that series booked his passage to

Australia the following winter where he unceremoniously had his box turned inside out by Jeff Thomson at Perth. His ability to play spin on that tour was scarcely put to the test.

On reflection Zimbabweans were never going to come to terms with Lloyd. He was quite unlike anything they had ever experienced. His humour and accent were as incomprehensible to them as a broad Glaswegian Scot might be to me. His mood on the Under-19 tour did not endear him to the locals so the Zimbabweans certainly weren't going to lift a finger to help when he returned with the senior England team towards the end of 1996.

Despite all the energy and innovation of his coaching style, the tour of Zimbabwe began badly. Practice facilities were limited and warm-up matches lost or poorly played. It did not take long for confidence to seep away and reach a very low ebb. The Zimbabweans were understandably cock-a-hoop and revelled somewhat in our misery, as well they might. To make matters worse, Mike Atherton had been laid low by the recurrence of a back injury which would ultimately curtail his career. Lloyd's strong brew and whirlwind approach were not at this stage having the desired effect upon team morale. "Today," he said in one of his more ebullient team talks, "you're going to play as you've never played before: ... well." It got a laugh if nothing else.

Lloyd so wanted the players to fulfil their potential. He really did believe in them. He had stoical faith that they would come good sooner or later, but it wasn't until we shifted our base camp from the stuffy and oppressive confines of Harare to the fresh air and wide streets of Bulawayo that spirits began to lift a little. We travelled about the town in a girls' high school bus, a feature that did not go unnoticed by the press but, notwithstanding this minor setback, there was a jollier hue about the faces of the players. Lloyd even took some of them – not me – to the local line-dancing club for an evening's entertainment.

After much ado and a fair amount of failure, the inaugural Test match was played shortly before Christmas in Bulawayo. The weather was fine; the pitch looked good and the ground a pleasing throw-back to the colonial past. Zimbabwe, a more than useful side and with nothing to lose, were playing against a fragile and slightly bruised England party whose normal joie de vivre had been squeezed a little dry. It was anybody's game.

The match smouldered gently until suddenly it sprang to life on the final afternoon when England, up against it for much of the time, were set 205 runs to win in what amounted to 37 overs. After the lacklustre build-up to the Test series, it now seemed England had a real chance to win. Whilst putting his pads on to bat, Atherton gave a fighting team talk which suggested England go hell for leather for the target. The pitch was firm and outfield a lot faster than those in Harare. Suddenly, and rather unexpectedly, it was tantalising stuff. Although Atherton was dismissed early, bowled by Olonga, Nick Knight and Alec Stewart quickly took the initiative and began to punish both pace and spin. Their exhilarating partnership took England to within 50 runs of the target but, with time and overs running out, both wickets and momentum were forfeited. Amidst the hubbub and excitement that only five days of Test cricket can conjure up, five runs were needed from Heath Streak's last three balls. Knight could not score from the first of them, he ran two off the next; then, off the last, he was run out attempting the winning third run. It brought to an end a remarkable match – a glorious draw, many would say.

The repercussions were as dramatic and exciting as the match itself. The crowd, some 4,000 passionate Zimbabwean supporters, spilled onto the outfield, waving flags and embracing each other. The players shook hands and left the field in dignified fashion, cheered and mobbed on their way. It was a happy scene, played out as the sun sank low behind the trees. The players were physically and emotionally drained. Knight returned to the dressing room exhausted and in need of attention. There the atmosphere was muted as pangs of disappointment seeped into the hearts and lungs of players deprived of the reward they felt they rightfully deserved. All the same, it had been a great match for cricket and especially Zimbabwe who had achieved in just one encounter more than they could ever have wished. The script could hardly have been bettered.

Meanwhile, as the run chase was building up, Lloyd had taken himself off round the ground for a walk. Coaches often do this. It's a way of letting off steam and calming the nerves. Except in this case it didn't. As the hot afternoon wore on and into the evening, Lloyd got increasingly het up and agitated as the match began to reach its climax. His mood was not helped by the crowd who egged him on with much inevitable banter and many jocular words. He got into a real state and not even John Emburey, our patient and immensely calm assistant coach, could soothe him or even help put on the brakes. Zimbabweans and Lloyd never did see eye to eye, and by the time the match reached its conclusion he was beginning to boil over. Given half a chance, Atherton would have locked him away in the coach's room, had there been one, with a cold flannel wrapped round his forehead and with orders to stay there. He never got that chance.

As it was, formalities had to be completed. The dressing room was quiet, a mixture of elation, disappointment and, in the case of Knight, sheer exhaustion. Inevitably there was some murmuring about wides that should have been signalled, but all that was now in the past. The immediate future threw up the routine post-Test match press conference, rarely a jolly affair even at the best of times which this palpably was not.

"Come on, Athers," I said, "it's time to go. Where's Bumble?"

Lloyd had not been seen by the players all afternoon and he eventually returned to the dressing room, looking pale and angry, with Emburey. Once reunited, the three of us – Lloyd, Barclay and Atherton – trudged off to the dining room where the meeting was being held. It was a hot and clammy affair, no air at all, with dictaphones littered about on the table in front of us. After a few casual words from me about what a fine match it had been, and one to be remembered for years to come by all who saw it, we got down to business. Atherton, in answer to a question about his poor form, was doing his best to explain that he was feeling more confident by the day and it was nothing that a big score wouldn't put right, when, all of a sudden and without introduction, Lloyd, with no provocation and not following any logical train of thought, unexpectedly blurted out, "We murdered 'em, we flippin' murdered 'em." It was a startling revelation and took everyone by surprise. After a short pause he said it again and Martin Johnson, then of the *Independent* newspaper, was moved to point out that the match had in fact been drawn. As you might imagine, everything else about the day was quickly forgotten. The press had their headline and were now clambering over each other to reach their new lap-tops. This was too good a story to be shovelled under the carpet.

Damage limitation is probably where successive England managers have most experience. Over the years there have been enough disasters and diplomatic incidents to test the patience of Henry Kissinger. I suppose this was only a blip really but one which upset the sensitive nature of the Zimbabweans and made English cricket look rather silly.

The next day most of the team took the chance to visit Victoria Falls on their way back to Harare for the Test match immediately after Christmas. The Zimbabweans were thrilled that we were able to see just a little bit of their beloved country and especially this quite remarkable force of nature. Meanwhile I hired a car in Bulawayo and drove Atherton and Lloyd back to Harare and cleared the air somewhat on the way. The journey took all day so gave us much time for reflection.

Lloyd is a deeply passionate man, emotional and at times almost too honest for his own good; a brilliant communicator when behind the microphone in the commentary box or speaking after dinner. His empathy and understanding of an audience are outstanding, his use of language exceptional and timing superb. In some ways he's a bit of a genius, but calmness and serenity were not really his thing despite the inspiring nature of his character. Yet, amongst his sporting qualities, he is also an unusually fine fisherman – persevering, skilful and patient.

He became a regular member of our fishing team which travelled north to Scotland each September in pursuit of the elusive salmon. Atherton, Wingfield Digby, Barclay and Lloyd were the senior players in a party of diverse talents but great determination. Lloyd would still be there flogging the water when the rest of us had long since given up and retired for a drink. One lunchtime he caught a 14lb salmon while we were seeking consolation in the pub. Lloyd was gritty in all weathers and knew his stuff too.

Some years ago we hired a camper-van to make up for scanty accommodation in Aberdeenshire; Atherton and I quickly took refuge in the local pub. All went well for a while until one night,

when we were invited by our hosts to dinner in their castle nearby, Wingfield Digby's dogs ran wild and trashed, ravaged and seriously messed the van – horrible. Lloyd was inconsolable and so upset by the occurrence that he set off forthwith for home, albeit I think to a lucrative dinner engagement (an earner) and has never been back to Scotland since – which is a pity because, amongst his many talents, is his cooking. Nobody made fires better or indeed cooked fillets of beef more succulently than Lloyd. His culinary activity and quick wit have been much missed north of the border for too long.

In amongst all his funny ways – he was never ever dull – Lloyd left his mark upon coaching. He was at the forefront of innovation and experimentation with new ideas in the late 1990s. He challenged players to improve their game in ways hitherto unheard of. In those days there was less help and support close to hand – he did most things himself. He was chosen as head coach because it was felt a new style was needed, one based on enthusiasm and energy and up-to-date thinking. As it turned out it probably wasn't the perfect marriage, but it certainly pointed the way for what was to follow. To some extent Lloyd played the part of a modern-day John the Baptist and used his vision to pave the way for Duncan Fletcher's successful reign from the turn of the century.

Basil Lewis D'Oliveira

Born: Cape Town, South Africa, 4 October 1931
Died: Rushwick, Worcester, 18 November 2011

44 Tests for England (1966-1972)
2,484 runs at an average of 40.06, 5 centuries
47 wickets at an average of 39.55

367 first-class matches (1962-1980)
19,490 runs at an average of 40.26, 45 centuries
551 wickets at an average of 27.45

Basil D'Oliveira was already 33 years old when he played his first summer of county cricket – though at the time he only admitted to being 30. Deprived of a first-class career by the brutal Apartheid policy of his native South Africa, where he was classified a Cape Coloured, he came to England as the result of a recommendation by John Arlott.

That first full summer with Worcestershire, in 1965, was a great success. He finished sixth in the national batting averages, he took useful wickets with his medium-pace change bowling, and the county won the Championship. The next summer he became a regular for England.

He was a powerful batsman, with a short back-lift and a temperament for the big occasion, which he demonstrated emphatically when recalled to the England side to play Australia at The Oval in 1968. Spurred on by the prospect of touring his native country, he hit a magnificent 158, only for the selectors to overlook his claim to a tour place.

Through all the ensuing furore D'Oliveira kept his own counsel. He played a major part in England's Ashes triumph of 1970/71, and he lived to see a post-Apartheid South Africa return to the cricketing fold, playing their Tests against England for the Basil D'Oliveira Trophy.

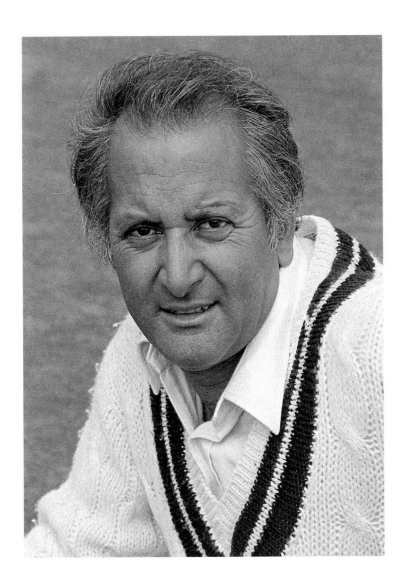

Basil D'Oliveira

It was still quite early on Friday morning when my mother dropped us – my best friend and me – at Brighton Station. This was a new adventure and quite an excitement too for two 14-year-olds. We were travelling to London, to The Oval, to watch the second day's play in England's final Test match against Australia in 1968. A queue for rail tickets, a bag of cheese-and-onion crisps, a can of something and we were on our way bound for Clapham Junction. The sun shone and anticipation grew. Although we were not quite sure which way to turn upon alighting at the station in South London, we need not have worried. "Just follow the crowd," I said to my friend which we did. A short bus ride and there we were outside The Oval and immersed in that unrivalled atmosphere that serves as a prelude to Test match cricket, the orchestra as it were tuning up prior to performance – scorecards, souvenirs, rosettes, salesmen of all sorts selling their wares amidst the dust and heat of South London.

The Oval was a scruffy place in the '60s, nothing smart or ostentatious and certainly no pretensions to grandeur. As we found our seats at the Vauxhall End and sat down with our backs to the gasometers, the ground seemed to me everything it should be in a rough old bit of Lambeth. After a particularly good opening day with the bat, we hoped to watch England continue its innings with Edrich, who had already passed a hundred, and D'Oliveira, well established in the 20s, at the crease.

This would be my first glimpse of D'Oliveira, whose glamorous name rather suggested success. Tall he seemed, much taller than Edrich, with an air of serenity and calmness which made him appear unhurried by the tempo of Test cricket. And yet, once into his stride, he struck the ball with unexpected power without much flapping of bat or flailing of arms. At the crease he stood remarkably still, upright and composed, and then allowed human nature to take over.

His innings of 158, though not without blemish, was crafted with style and a touch of class. With Edrich (who made a fine

164), Milburn, Dexter, Cowdrey and Graveney in the line-up, I just hadn't expected D'Oliveira to play the innings of his life. Not only had this been one of the great Test match displays, it had also played England into a powerful position from which to dictate the course of the match. The journey home was a happy one; I have had a soft spot for The Oval ever since.

Four days later, sitting on a cliff top in Cornwall and gazing far out to sea, I listened to Arlott, Gibson and possibly Alston describe the final hour's play of that match on the radio. On a drying pitch Underwood had the Australians on the run, and it was only at the last gasp that he trapped Inverarity lbw to win the match and so square the rubber. But it was the repercussions of D'Oliveira's remarkable innings that were to cause such a rumpus for cricket in the months following.

*

Although D'Oliveira's name would be much in the news over the next two years, I didn't come across him again until four years later when I played against him for Sussex versus Worcestershire. While the storm had swept all about D'Oliveira's shoulders he had remained remarkably impassive, refusing to be dragged into an ugly political mess over South Africa. It may well have been that he didn't have a political bone in his body but, throughout the growing crisis which clearly exposed the South African government for what it was, he kept his counsel and composure to such an extent that, as an 18-year-old, I rather wondered what all the fuss had been about. After all D'Oliveira, by my way of thinking, had quite a pale complexion in comparison with the likes of Seymour

Nurse or Wesley Hall and certainly not in the least bit black by most standards.

He was bowling when I strode out to bat at number ten for Sussex, with firm instructions to have a slog for an extra batting bonus point. Although D'Oliveira didn't bowl fast, he did bowl very straight, a man dedicated to the philosophy of unerring accuracy. It only took one ball; I swished blindly across the line and missed; that was it, given out lbw to D'Oliveira by Bill Alley, the umpire, first ball for 0.

The match fizzled out into the sort of dull draw which did little to lift the morale of County Championship cricket but, just before stumps were drawn, I reached a notable milestone in my brief career. Although I had by now played in some seven first-class matches and bowled nearly sixty overs, mostly in short spells, I had yet to take a wicket and was beginning to wonder whether this was a feat altogether beyond me. I was brought on to bowl in Worcestershire's second innings, more to boost the Sussex over rate while the match reached its dreary conclusion than anything else. Glenn Turner and Ted Hemsley were batting; the members were dozing off, and all was quiet at Hove's County Ground. But then, out of the blue, I bowled an attempted swinger to Turner, and indeed it did drift away from him in the air towards Tony Greig fielding at slip. Turner propped forward as he did on many occasions. The ball hit the pitch and nipped back sharply towards the groping Turner and found its way between bat and pad to clip the top of the off stump. Titmus or Illingworth would have been proud of such a malevolent ball. To me it was a minor miracle, a heaven-sent gift to lend some purpose to a dying match. Turner, bowled Barclay 26. Greig clapped his hands enthusiastically and shouted, "You'll never bowl a better ball than that in your career." He was right.

*

I didn't know D'Oliveira very well, hardly at all in fact by contrast to the other subjects of this book. But he had an aura about him which had nothing to do with the mildly tanned colour of his skin around which the world of cricket was briefly torn apart. He stood tall at over six foot and was upright in posture. Unhurried and with a calm, placid countenance, he was slightly greying at the temples, suggesting he was no youngster when he first embarked upon his cricketing career. Unflappable and not one for making explosive movements, he stood very still in his stance and simply used his talent to hit the ball cleanly. Never, so far as I am aware, did he allow himself to be dragged into the row surrounding his colour and South African politics. My impression was that he let the whole grisly business wash over him like the surf in the sea. He simply bobbed up the other side and got on with what he was good at.

I encountered him again in 1974 at Hastings, the year in which Worcestershire won the County Championship. Once again he trapped me lbw although this time I had lasted a little longer. On returning to the small pavilion I turned to John Snow and said, "Quite unplayable, that D'Oliveira is; the ball wobbled both ways in the air before I missed it." Snow replied, "Don't be silly, he's not that good."

Five years later in 1979 D'Oliveira, despite his age, was still playing for Worcestershire. It may even be that I hastened his retirement. He came in to bat in Worcestershire's first innings at number six, a little more portly, thinning grey hair and slightly stiff of limb but still upright and motionless in stance. I was bowling and, by my standards, having a good day with three wickets already in the bag including Glenn Turner, albeit for 118.

Early in D'Oliveira's innings I bowled him a short ball wide of the off stump – a long hop, to be precise. Nonetheless I was in attacking mode – a silly point and two short-legs in place, despite D'Oliveira's reputation as a hard hitter of spinners. Anyway his eyes lit up when he spotted this tasty morsel coming his way; he set himself on the back foot and fairly cracked the ball into the off-side where it would surely have proceeded fast in the direction of the Cathedral and River Severn, had Peter Graves's knee not stood in its way. Instead of reaching the boundary the ball ricocheted high up in the air towards extra cover to cries of "Catch it", which indeed I did, hurling myself with a well-timed dive to claim an unlikely catch.

D'Oliveira, caught and bowled Barclay 2. It looked quite distinguished in the newspaper the following day.

Expressionless and resigned to his fate, D'Oliveira trudged back to the pavilion, accompanied by Graves who was carried off by several players. In its own way it had been an unexpectedly destructive delivery.

D'Oliveira didn't play another match that summer. I think this dismissal must have been the last straw. He announced his retirement not long afterwards.

Imran Khan Niazi

Born: Lahore, Pakistan, 25 November 1952

88 Tests for Pakistan (1971-1992)
3,807 runs at an average of 37.69, 6 centuries
362 wickets at an average of 22.81
48 Tests as captain

382 first-class matches (1969-1992)
17,771 runs at an average of 36.79, 30 centuries
1,287 wickets at an average of 22.32

Imran Khan captained Pakistan with considerable success between 1982 and 1992. Traditionally a country which had lost more Tests than it had won, they were defeated in only eight of his 48 matches in charge. In his final game as a professional cricketer he crowned it all by leading Pakistan to victory in the World Cup final in Melbourne in 1992.

He was a fast-bowling all-rounder who completed the "triple double" of 3,000 runs and 300 wickets in just 75 Tests, a feat which only Ian Botham, in 72, has achieved in fewer matches. His 62 wickets in nine Tests in the calendar year of 1982 were taken at an average of 13.29, the lowest by any bowler taking 50 Test wickets in a year.

He played for Sussex from 1977 to 1988. In 131 matches for the county he averaged 43 with the bat and under 20 with the ball, figures which make him among the greatest all-rounders in the history of the county game.

After cricket he entered public life in Pakistan. In memory of his mother he raised funds to build a specialist cancer hospital in Lahore. Then he entered politics, forming a new party and being elected to parliament in 2002. As this book goes to press in 2013, he is one of the leading candidates in his country's election.

Imran Khan

Not long ago I had a dream. A strange one. Dreams usually are. I was standing on the bridge spanning the River Test at Stockbridge and staring intently at the stream of clear water below as the mayflies, in little clouds, danced joyfully in their mating ritual before collapsing upon the current to lay their eggs and die. A large black car drew up beside me. Imran Khan opened the back door and hailed me with a friendly welcome, "Hello Johnny," that's what he called me – we were quite good chums – "jump in," he said, "my driver is taking me to see John Woodcock at Longparish just a few miles upstream." Imran knows all about rivers having once written a book about the mighty Indus in Pakistan, illustrated by stunning photographs. So I did as I was bid, and we set off through lanes lined with hedges and water meadows glowing in the late spring sunshine. Before long we arrived at John Woodcock's cottage opposite the church. To our surprise there was quite a party in progress and a fire burning in the grate. Woodcock had been looking forward to seeing Imran again and so had, rather surprisingly, invited his friends in from the village, mostly middle-aged women, old dears you might say, to meet him.

Despite the early hour, more like tea time, they were all drinking champagne and by the sound of it were well into their second glass when we arrived. The driver parked the car, and we were both ushered in warmly by Woodcock who quickly planted a glass of refreshing bubbles into each of our hands. Imran, a confirmed non-drinker in real life, accepted his with gusto. He, I knew of old, easily gets bored and tires of social niceties quickly. Not on this occasion, however, he was quite the life and soul of the party, happily accepting a second glass of champagne. Cricket was hardly discussed. The local folk from Longparish were more interested in Imran the politician and how his Campaign for Justice might make a difference in the turbulent world of Pakistan. "I shall win," he proclaimed somewhat immodestly, possibly by then under the influence of his third glass, "because I am brave." All of a sudden he bared his left arm and showed it to his enraptured audience. "See that," he said, pointing to an impressive scar just above the elbow, "I got that fighting a man-eating tiger in the Bengal jungle, got the

178

better of him as you can see." When Imran got going he could tell a good story which might be a helpful omen for his career in politics.

As if not satisfied by this tale of courage and heroism, Imran then took his audience by surprise when he proceeded to kiss each one of them roundly on the lips. They did not seem dissatisfied and I think put it down to the passion of a man with a mission. Presumably these were campaigning tactics to which Pakistan was well used. We were in the midst of saying our thank-yous and goodbyes when I woke up.

For most of us dreams never come true, and I'm sure this dream won't disturb the statistics either. Real life is rather different. For instance, Imran did injure his arm but not at the claws of a man-eating tiger, or a great white shark for that matter. No, the truth was more mundane, though endearing none the less. He slipped, as a youngster in Lahore, while climbing a tree and broke his arm when trying to cling on to a branch. His arm was badly set at the local hospital and as a result left him with an impressive scar upon which he has dined out ever since.

To understand Imran at all requires a lot of patience and imagination. He could be impulsive and yet measured too – both reliable and less so within the same hour. He is an idealist, totally inspired at times and admirably persevering. Without doubt his mother's illness and subsequent death filled him with a greater purpose for his life beyond cricket. His captaincy of Pakistan and success in the World Cup in 1992 was the summit of his achievements on the cricket field. An all-rounder to rival even Sobers and Botham, he could have done just about anything following his retirement, but instead he set his heart upon raising money for and establishing The Shauket Khanum Memorial Cancer Hospital and research centre in 1996 as a memorial to his mother. I am sure his success in the field of medicine inspired him to take up the cudgel and enter the dangerous and fickle world of Pakistan's politics.

I saw him rather differently when he arrived from Worcester to play for Sussex in the late '70s and early '80s. Despite his virtuosity as a player there was a certain naïve enthusiasm that accompanied his talent and heroic performances. But without doubt he had his irritating moments. Some of the Sussex team would tire of his aristocratic manner and apparent aloofness. "Cor, skip, you let him do anything," Colin Wells would moan, and indeed Imran was constantly late and rarely cleaned his boots. But, on the whole, we put up with him. He always tried hard and was very proud of his own game. It mattered to him, and he was sensitive about press reports that might get into the Pakistan newspapers. He practised as hard as anyone in the team, almost permanently walking about with his pads on as if aware of Sussex's batting frailties.

Imran was always keen to improve and worked tirelessly on his technique, with both bat and ball. Soon after his arrival at Sussex, and perhaps influenced by advice and encouragement from John Snow, his bowling action took on a more sideways shape, accompanied by a large jump prior to his delivery stride. He thus became a genuinely fast bowler but initially, carried away by the pace of Hove's green pitches, would bowl too short. He loved to see the ball whizz through to the wicket-keeper while the batsman ducked. Later in his career he corrected this and learnt to pitch the ball up and swing it both ways – absolutely lethal. I used him ruthlessly, determined, as I was then, to squeeze all the potential out of his ability. "Oh please, Immy," I'd say to him, "could you bear the thought of bowling two more overs? I think it could win us the match and you can then go to London for a break." This usually did the trick, and it didn't take him long to melt, "Oh Johnny, for you I'll do it just this time."

When he batted he became nervous and over-excited. "Oh God," he would say with his head in his batting gloves, "I cannot play Pocock *[off-spinner Pat Pocock from Surrey]* – give me 20 runs, God, please give me 20." Strangely enough the rest of us weren't so worried about Pocock; he might get you out but at least he bowled slowly and you were safe. Our fears were much more acutely centred upon the fearsome prospect of Sylvester Clarke bowling very fast from the other end.

Imran could rarely be relied upon for consistency of mood. Up one moment, down the next. He could shift from super-confident to "Oh God" in a matter of seconds. At Derby one day early in June we were competing in the Benson and Hedges Cup quarter-finals, a luxury not often afforded to Sussex who rarely peaked early in the season. Derbyshire didn't fare too well, and we bowled them out quite cheaply. Back in the pavilion Imran sat down with a triumphant and confident look on his face, accompanied by a sheepish grin, and said, "Today, Johnny I would like to open the batting; I feel it is my day." I conceded to his request and made the necessary adjustments which meant I had to drop down the batting order myself. That didn't bother me much. Ten minutes later out went Imran to bat, swinging his arms about like Botham, with Mendis. Imran survived his first ball. The second, bowled by Oldham, just drifted away from Imran's bat but not enough to prevent the ball touching the outside edge and flying off at a comfortable height to Miller at slip who took the catch. 0 for 1, Khan out second ball. As befits disaster, all was quiet in the dressing room when he returned. He was quite calm. After he had put down his bat and removed his pads amidst stifled laughter from Gould in another corner, he looked at me and simply said, "Johnny, I don't think that was a very good idea." With that he bid us farewell – I'm sure he stayed long enough to see us win the match – and joined the Pakistan team for their 1982 tour of England.

It was not always like that, very often the opposite in fact. Imran found one-day cricket and especially the 40-over Sunday variety very tedious. Instead of the usual unimaginative approach of protecting boundaries right from the beginning (there were fewer, if any, restrictions then), Imran suggested that we used his

181

few overs for an all-out attack and thus startle the opposition. He was right; it did. Batsmen well used to a peaceful Sunday afternoon with church bells in the background were suddenly and unexpectedly subjected to a full-scale assault. Three slips were the order of the day. Essex, a fine side, were our first victims. I think we bowled them out for 115. "You'll never keep it up," Fletcher, Essex's captain, said to me afterwards. He was right, of course, but that year, 1982, we did win the Sunday League Trophy with a record number of points and enjoyed it all the more for our ambitious approach. As a side line, Le Roux was always a bit miffed that I didn't allow him as many slips as Imran. But, let's be honest, Imran was a true thoroughbred, possibly a Nijinsky to Le Roux's Red Rum. Le Roux was an out-and-out stayer, though not quite in Red Rum's class.

On another occasion, but a year later in 1983, we played an extraordinary match against Warwickshire at Edgbaston in August. Imran had been miserable all summer as well he might because he had been suffering from shin soreness, stress fractures which led to horribly aching legs and an irritable mind too. He was not happy. His specialist doctor prescribed that he could do some batting if he wanted to but no bowling. Later in the season the same doctor relented somewhat and suggested it might help to stimulate healing if Imran was to bowl up to four or five overs in a day, but no more. This presented quite a challenge for both me as captain and Imran as bowler – when to use this precious spell. Certainly not the new ball, Imran would waste that and anyway he was a far more awkward prospect with the older one. It needed careful planning, and on one occasion we got it dead right. The match in question was in Birmingham and beginning to drift away from us with time evaporating on the last day. "Come on, Immy, I think we can wait no more," I said, throwing him a rather aged and emaciated ball. "Good luck." He steamed in on his fragile shins like a man possessed. In 4.3 overs Imran destroyed what remained of Warwickshire's batting and finished with six for 6 on an otherwise dull day at Edgbaston. Unfortunately this remarkable spell showed no signs of accelerating the healing process, the reverse if anything.

Probably Imran's finest hour for Sussex came in a championship match played against Derbyshire at Eastbourne in August 1981. Why he should have chosen this game to perform at his supreme best, I don't know. For sure, he liked Eastbourne and often did well there. Indeed, once he brought his girlfriend, Emma Sargeant, a fine young artist, to watch him play. On that occasion he scored a serene hundred between lunch and tea while she sat cross-legged behind the marquees, oblivious to all activity on the field, and painted a view of the scene with the tent ropes in the foreground. Emma, during her all too brief appearance in Imran's life, became quite a friend, not so much of mine but more of my wife, Mary-Lou, with whom she whiled away the time at cricket matches, giggling and laughing irreverently, for her life was of a Bohemian nature.

This time, though, the match really mattered. Sussex were chasing hard at the top of the County Championship table and a victory against Derbyshire would keep us in the hunt. For two days the match ambled along slowly while spectators, enjoying their holidays, ate their picnics basking in the sunshine, much as they would by the seaside just a few hundred yards away. Even on the final day the match was still sliding ominously towards a stalemate when an unlikely twist in the plot emerged, at a stage quite unexpected for both players and crowd.

So far as I can remember, Colin Wells, a man more used to bowling at a brisk medium pace, was trying out his occasional leg spinners. David Steele was the batsman. He had scored a few runs by this stage and was well into his stride. He was happy as anything, in his element in fact, to be tapping gentle half-volleys back to the bowler. The game was going nowhere, and a dull draw was in the offing. The Sussex players were littered unstrategically about the field, all of them bored, and beginning to plan their routes from Eastbourne to Nottingham, our next destination. "Through Polegate on to Streatham, then Vauxhall Bridge, quick snack, Hendon Way, M1 and off." This was the tenor of the conversation being whispered around the covers as the next stage in a cricketer's life unfolded – travel – how to get from A to B, without too much delay.

Imran was fielding on the football field at deep square leg beneath the huge town hall clock. He was a long way from me at slip, but I could hear him muttering restlessly and fretfully. Eventually, after yet another Wells over, he ran over to me with passion in his face, "I can't stand this any longer," he said, "I am going to bowl." "Good heavens," I replied, "when?" "Now," he shouted and began to run off the field to change from his plimsolls into his bowling boots. By the time Wells had bowled one more over, Imran was ready and before too long was steaming in past the umpire, Lofty Herman, who, up until then, was enjoying a quiet and peaceful afternoon in the sun. After a ball or two Ian Gould, our wicket-keeper, turned to me at slip and said, "Skip, it's swinging." "That's strange, isn't it, for such an old ball?" I replied. The new ball was available and had been for some time, but both Imran and Gould had given me a funny look when I suggested that use of the new ball might give us our last chance.

To reduce the length of the story, I can tell you that Imran took four wickets in five balls and in so doing bowled out the remaining Derbyshire batsman. This left us with the tricky target of 234 runs to win the match. As we walked off the field with stunned expressions on our faces, Imran called me over. "I want to bat number three," he said, "I feel inspired and can't wait any longer." Although I pointed out that it didn't normally take the Sussex batting long to get down to number four, he was insistent. I made the necessary adjustments without too much confrontation in the dressing room, and it wasn't long before Imran was striding in to bat. While batsmen fell to the left and right of him, Imran proceeded to play the innings of his life. It was his day. At 104 for 5 it appeared that the Sussex ship was severely holed and going down fast. Parker, who had got out earlier, had already consumed two beers on the balcony and was now into a third and beginning to make quite a noise as the match began to erupt. In 80 minutes Imran scored 107 runs, and we won with just five balls to spare.

If I could relive just one day in my career ... this would be it. On that Friday in Eastbourne I learnt more than ever before about human nature, frailties and triumphs, as well as reverse swing which had always been a bit of a mystery to me. I never really understood it – I didn't have to. Imran had mastered it, and Gould was always good enough to keep me informed.

Leadership can't have been easy for Imran. After all he was a performer of such supreme talent that to think of the needs of others could not have come naturally to him. And yet he took on the complex web of intrigue that represents Pakistan cricket. His style at the time suited the country, and he had in his armoury just about the most talented and explosive batsman since the war in Javed Miandad. Abdul Qadir too, a little genius in his own right, proved some time before Shane Warne that leg spin could be a very potent force in world cricket. But Imran had to make it all work. Whether or not his experiences in England shaped his thinking I don't know, but it certainly gave him confidence and perhaps made him less selfish. I don't write this as a criticism. All cricketers, very much including me, are selfish. We are all committed to the cause and, in so doing, often think little of others. Imran would have quickly discovered that, as captain, he would have to become more of a giver and less of a taker as well as understanding the importance of both and the difference as well.

In politics his success will be measured by what he can do for others. The natural and instinctive tendency towards selfishness will have to give way to unselfishness. I have my doubts but wouldn't anybody? However, Imran will never cease to surprise; he did so on the cricket field and could well do the same in the larger world. His shyness may pose a problem for him because it can at times make him appear somewhat aloof or even arrogant. He will need to acquire the common touch, if he has not already done so, an essential quality for him to succeed in the front line. If I were to be bold enough to give him any advice, I would say: hold to your policy, be true to yourself and inspire trust. Given those attributes I think he's got half a chance of making an impact.

185

Ian Charter MacLaurin

Born: Blackheath, Kent, 30 March 1937

Ian MacLaurin was a talented cricketer, a good enough batsman to spend five years in the Malvern College XI (two as captain) and to play for Kent 2nd XI and Hertfordshire.

After school and National Service he joined Tesco in 1959 as a management trainee, rising to the board in 1970 and becoming first Managing Director, then in 1985 Chairman. He stayed in post till 1997, by which time the company had refocused its business so successfully that it had overtaken Sainsbury's as the country's leading supermarket.

Subsequently he spent several years as Chairman of Vodafone.

In 1996 he was appointed Chairman of the England and Wales Cricket Board, given the task of overseeing a major review of the domestic game and its relationship with the national team. He produced a report, Raising the Standard, *which set in motion many of the changes that have since taken effect: the two-division County Championship, the central contracts for England players and the structure of regional pyramids in club cricket.*

In 1996 he was created a life peer, taking the title of Baron MacLaurin of Knebworth.

Ian MacLaurin

Ian MacLaurin, between 1996 and 2003, had a profound and creative influence upon the world of cricket after he was elected to chair the newly formed England and Wales Cricket Board (ECB). A capable minor counties and club cricketer himself, he was the first hard-nosed and thick-skinned businessman to throw his heart and soul into the entrenched world of professional and recreational cricket. Coming from a background where his business expertise could hardly contemplate failure or sloppy performances, I imagine that MacLaurin must have been quite taken aback, and indeed out of his depth, when he first encountered an organisation the like of which he had never seen before.

Having built up Tesco from a small-time grocer to a multinational chain of stylish supermarkets, the new cricket board by comparison must have felt like a cottage industry to MacLaurin. And yet I believe his heart was very much in the game; he had an instinct for it, but his approach was to be very different from the past which inevitably took a few people by surprise. After all, he was not a man who made friends easily nor did he readily seek them. He didn't say much and seemed at times to belong to some special silent order in which speech and subsequent goodwill played only a small part.

Austere and quite shy he was, and intimidating too. He inspired both fear and respect in equal measure – a bit Thatcher-like in some ways – but at the same time he was very much a doer, a man of action, but not in the least bit cosy or comfortable to be with. He wouldn't want any of that sort of thing to compromise or cramp his style. As with Tesco he preferred to succeed or fail through the delivery of results.

For some years cricket had trundled along under the combined forces of the Test and County Cricket Board and National Cricket Association, responsible for the professional and recreational game respectively. Under the ECB all this was to become more streamlined and accountable. Very gradually a different style of management began to emerge, and the counties came to realise that things would never be quite the same again. MacLaurin was just the man to take on this challenge. He was a good listener. He came into the job as a relative outsider and therefore with a clean sheet and a clear view. He was by no means everybody's cup of tea; charm was not his strong point and, although he didn't have the gift of the gab, he had the most incisive mind and got the nub of the matter in hand quicker than anyone I knew. He was directed towards his goal by a determination to do the right thing for the game and its participants. I imagine that his past experiences must have influenced his thinking considerably, but MacLaurin quickly realised that cricket, essentially a game involving thousands of volunteers, could not be ruled with the same toughness and precision that would be common in the corporate world. And so MacLaurin had to adapt his style to this new role.

It took a while for him to clear away some of the debris, but before too long a new plan for cricket was published under the title *Raising the Standard*. It was written in simple language and short sentences, its objective being to give the country something upon which to hang its hat. But in it, above all, MacLaurin realised that English cricket needed to tackle its problems from the top downwards. A successful Test match and one-day team was essential if the game was to have any chance of financing itself with confidence for future generations. All standards had to be driven up.

If I have so far painted MacLaurin as a rather stern and severe man, it is because that is how he appeared to me on our first meeting. In those early days he didn't smile often, and his dark eyes rarely lit up, cleverly concealing his innermost thoughts. He kept his own counsel and didn't let many people ruffle his feathers. I first encountered him in 1990 when we sat opposite each other in the MCC Committee Room at Lord's. It was my first full committee meeting. Lord Griffiths, a man of great intellect and humour, was President that year, and the main topic on the agenda concerned the vexed problem of whether ladies should be admitted to the hitherto all-male enclave of MCC. It was quite a hot potato for starters. Griffiths, who never took his eye off the ball for one moment but also conducted the debate with a smile, went round the room and allowed everyone to say their piece. I was very nervous when it came to my turn to make my maiden offering amongst such distinguished company. I spoke up, though, in favour of the ladies. I like women on the whole, and I have a feeling MacLaurin's vote – he likes women too – went the same way. The result, though, was inconclusive. Eight votes to seven, one way or the other. I think both sides settled for a draw.

During the early '90s and some time before MacLaurin became Chairman of ECB, both of us spent several years on the MCC Committee. I don't remember MacLaurin contributing to debates all that often and neither did I, but when he did, people listened; they pricked up their ears as well they might for, when MacLaurin spoke, his style was succinct and clear. He had a way of getting to the heart of the matter in just a few words, rarely allowing humour to cloud the issue.

Apart from those MCC meetings where we scarcely met, I didn't bump into MacLaurin again until late 1996 when the England team was assembled at the Copthorne Hotel, prior to departure from Gatwick to Zimbabwe. Amidst last-minute goodbyes and tearful farewells to families, Ian MacLaurin and Tim Lamb, his chief executive, bustled about amongst players who were distracted by much cricket bat-signing and the like, so probably not fully concentrating on the good luck wishes as much as they should. Departure is a tense and emotional business, not to be taken lightly nor for the faint-hearted.

Back in the summer, notwithstanding the disastrous World Cup campaign in India and Pakistan the previous February and March, for which I had been assistant manager, I had been appointed to manage the latest England campaign to Zimbabwe and then onwards to New Zealand. David Lloyd was head coach and John Emburey his assistant. MacLaurin must have viewed the combination of Barclay, an enthusiastic and friendly part-timer, and David Lloyd, a dedicated if slightly wild coach, with some suspicion. It could not possibly have been what he was used to from his senior management days at Tesco.

If performances were anything to go by, MacLaurin and Lamb must have spent the cold early days of December with their heads in their hands as the press broke story upon story of woeful news.

It was too much for them, of course; before too long they had to come out to Harare to see for themselves, which indeed they did just after Christmas.

They were greeted by a pretty motley crew. By that stage we had drawn the first Test match in Bulawayo when, at the end, the scores were level after England had turned the tables on Zimbabwe with a thrilling run chase. Briefly, sanity was restored – but was quickly followed by Lloyd's "We murdered 'em" episode at the press conference. This set us back a bit as we lost further ground in the public relations stakes. With the exception of the final day of this Test match, the England team had scarcely distinguished itself either on or off the field. The second Test match was due to start on Boxing Day in sultry weather and was accompanied by the heavy atmosphere of a team which was imbued with neither good spirit nor joie de vivre. MacLaurin and Lamb's arrival coincided with the second day's play when England were already struggling to come to terms with a slow pitch and even slower outfield.

MacLaurin, while in Harare, took the opportunity to talk to as many people as possible, including me, about the state of English cricket. A man of few words himself, he listened so well that you were never quite sure that he had absorbed the information imparted. He tended to stare ahead with fixed eyes which induced the speaker to fill the gaps with further talk and hurried observations, not always well thought out. I met him in my hotel room, and we chatted from some 45 minutes before he went off to play golf. He was smartly dressed and certainly looked the part in plus fours and long socks with red tags. He loved playing golf and still does, so far as I'm aware. I liked that. Even the most confident of men is bound to suffer at the hands of a game that demands so much humility at every turn. Golf does not let you get away with things; days spent thrashing away in the rough, and then missing short putts, put paid to that. I felt that, if MacLaurin played golf, there must be some good in him. I clung to that hope. With him sitting opposite me in my room, with a cup of coffee in hand, I felt nearly an equal and became quite relaxed as I told him about the disasters that had befallen the team. To some extent I was talking against myself and yet I warmed to the task as I went on. I felt it was helping both him and me – quite therapeutic in a way.

"You've obviously got too much on your plate," he said after a bit. I tried to explain that it wasn't as bad as that, but my words did not have much weight. From our chat it became quite clear that more back-up staff were needed to ensure that overseas tours ran more smoothly. MacLaurin was appalled that players at this level were still expected to share rooms. That had to stop, and indeed it did when we got to New Zealand. I can't believe our success there was due solely to this change of policy, but perhaps it helped. MacLaurin had many points to make, and he voiced them forcefully. He was also astonished that we didn't have a professional responsible for the management of the media, never an easy task at the best of times. Amateurism in a press conference was a recipe for disaster and gave the press a licence to run riot – which they did and still do, given half a chance. Editors will do anything for a story and the prospect of increasing sales. By the end of our meeting I felt cleansed to some extent and better able to tackle the climb ahead.

It can't have been easy for MacLaurin. He had been used to a highly operational board throughout his career and not one made up of part-timers, amateurs, and a handful of executives mostly steeped in the narrow and jealously protective world of first-class cricket. His instincts may have veered towards ruthlessness and bullying, but it was hard for him to apply these tactics to such amiable people. A balance had to be sought. In due course some fine men were appointed – Hugh Morris, John Carr and Alan Fordham, to name three. This set the ball in motion. I guess that MacLaurin fell out with many people in the process, especially the county committees and their chairmen. I doubt whether he endeared himself to them, and in all probability he didn't give a damn. He had been elected to do a job – what he believed to be right for English cricket – and nothing was going to stand in his way of having a crack at that.

Cricket needed someone like MacLaurin in the mid-1990s. As it turned out he was in the right place at the right time. The game was lucky to have him involved, however much he upset the apple cart. He had to steer his way along a path in which economic welfare and strength had to be balanced with cricketing requirements and necessities – not easy. Somehow he had to drag the bogged-down nature of the game along with him as he pushed forward. MacLaurin simply played the part of a tough trouble-shooter whose task it was to sharpen up the elite sector of English cricket so that its success would cascade down through the system. That was the idea.

MacLaurin never sought popularity, not someone you would necessarily choose to have dinner with, but he was in turn both pragmatic and professional and believed in ruthless efficiency from his staff. Amongst other things he championed the cause of central contracts, to be awarded to the country's top cricketers. This was never going to find total favour with the counties who had nurtured these players but, without doubt, over the years this policy has served both the players and the country's cricket well.

MacLaurin was feared by some while he intimidated others; he was not someone ruled by a warm heart but, despite this, he unquestionably helped pave the way for the successes of recent years. At the moment the England Test team has rarely been in better shape.

The problems and frailties of English cricket in 1996 suited MacLaurin. I believe he much enjoyed coming in from the outside and shaking it all up. He recognised a muddle when he saw one and was hell bent on sorting it out. There may have been little love lost between him and many stalwarts of the game, but cricket has been well pleased with the outcome.

Peter Moores

Born: Macclesfield, Cheshire, 18 December 1962

231 first-class matches (1983-1998)
7,351 runs at an average of 24.34, 7 centuries
502 catches and 44 stumpings

Peter Moores joined Sussex in 1985, taking over the wicket-keeping duties from Ian Gould two years later. He remained a regular member of the side for 11 summers, in the last of which – a tumultuous one after the overthrow of much of the club's hierarchy – he was captain.

He became the county's coach, a position in which he soon made his mark. Seven times in its history Sussex had finished as runners-up, yet in 2003, amid great South Coast celebrations, the team finally threw off the jinx by winning the County Championship.

Moores moved on to a role with the England National Cricket Academy, and in 2007 he was appointed successor to Duncan Fletcher as England's coach. After a very public fall-out with Kevin Pietersen, he left the post at the beginning of 2009.

Keeping his dignity, he returned to county cricket as coach at Lancashire. In 2011, amid the high excitement of a breathtaking run chase at Taunton, the little-fancied men of the North-West won their first outright Championship title for 77 years.

Peter Moores

Shane Warne, partly in jest but with a smidgen of irritation in his tone, once gave his views on coaching, admittedly with a grin on his face. He said something to this effect: "The best use of a coach is to drive you to and from the match."

Bearing in mind how much Terry Jenner had encouraged him throughout his career, this sentiment didn't totally endear him to the world of coaching. But it has inspired me to write a few words about a modern-day, up-to-date cricket coach and, in so doing, perhaps discuss how coaching and its relationship with the game have developed over the years and helped to improve the performances of players.

Without doubt the influence of the coach upon teams has increased enormously from the days when Micky Stewart took a grip upon Surrey as their first manager in 1979 and, a few years later, England – for whom he was something of a pioneer. Up until then coaching was still considered by some to be no more than a matter of transport – indeed, Micky was viewed with some suspicion by the old guard. They believed that players, once picked for England, should really know what they are about without being nannied along by an interfering coach keen to justify his existence. Times have, of course, changed and a succession of coaches have now succeeded Micky with varying degrees of success, Duncan Fletcher and Andy Flower so far the most notable for their achievements. Success requires a certain amount of skill, dexterity and luck, perhaps in equal measure. In this piece, I am going to write about Peter Moores, a great friend of mine, for whom luck did not leap to the rescue when he was given his chance to coach the England team in 2007.

At the time I felt he had good credentials to be England's coach – not a great player himself but a useful one, a wicket-keeper and so blessed with strong powers of concentration, the experience of one season as Sussex captain during which the county propped up the championship, and a wise knowledge of cricket's fickle nature where rarely does failure lurk far beneath the surface. Moores was not perfect himself – no suggestion of that. He would frequently get over-excited when he batted; a compulsive hooker, he got himself out playing loose shots and so could easily relate to fallibility. He could be stubborn, too. He was a solid wicket-keeper and became a fine coach of young keepers but, like the rest of us, would drop the occasional catch and so mar a good day. He had strong hands, but his acquaintance with the consequences of a mistake or two would later become one of the greatest strengths in his coaching career.

Moores' term as head coach with Sussex began in 1998 when he relinquished the responsibility of captaincy and handed over to Chris Adams, newly recruited from Derbyshire. In a way they were both lucky as they set out together from the bottom of the pile with only one way to go. As they got to know each other, it was the strength of this relationship that began to pave the way for future successes. The understanding between coach and captain marks the difference between the success and failure of a campaign, always assuming there are enough essential skills to get by with. At Sussex it worked; there would be occasional flare-ups as there are in any close family but, by and large, the foundations were strong and could withstand the odd ruction.

Together with his own experiences, Moores became the best qualified coach he could possibly be by taking on the challenge of a level four qualification from the England and Wales Cricket Board. He relished this opportunity, enjoyed it too and both contributed to and benefited from the course. He loved it. It was right up his street. And all this in a decade when new technology was progressively being used to monitor and support the game, and sports science becoming increasingly prominent. New training and fitness procedures were embraced, alongside the technical aspects of playing the game. A season crammed full of four and one-day matches was like fighting a war on two fronts. Moores was very much at home with this and threw his heart into it with immense gusto.

One of Moores' greatest attributes is that he has known what it is like to struggle. His playing career didn't coincide with a very successful Sussex team; things were a bit topsy-turvy at the time. When he arrived at Sussex in 1985, I was still captain and, although still a potent one-day side, we had diminished somewhat in the championship. I think he and I only played in one first-class match together – against Lancashire at Hastings. It was a game we ultimately won by bowling our opponents out after tea on the third day, but not before Jack Simmons had scored a hundred for Lancashire. At one stage during the hurly-burly of this tussle I rather startled Moores by turning to him from second slip and, despite it being his debut, asked him who he thought should bowl from the sea end. My question surprised him because it hadn't occurred to him that the captain would ask him about such important tactics. "Don't worry," Ian Greig piped up from first slip, "He always does that, goes round all in earshot until he gets the answer he wants. Consultation, that's what it's called."

Moores played just a handful of games in 1985 but early the following year was laid low by a serious and career-threatening injury to his back. I never quite knew what the problem was, but his back was successfully manipulated under anaesthetic; he was stranded in hospital for quite a while as he recovered. He was out of action throughout the summer of 1986, and for a time there were even doubts as to whether he would play again. But Peter, while not the most elegant of cricketers, was brave, determined and gritty, and also armed with a sense of humour and laughter which made up for a lot and helped him recover. Gradually he improved and his back became more mobile; once again he could bend his body and by the spring of 1987 he was back on his feet again. But I don't think he has ever forgotten those dark times when he was truly pole-axed. I am sure this setback concentrated his mind first as a player and later as a coach and gave him the insight to recognise the ups and downs of players for whom he was responsible. He knew all about setbacks and used that priceless asset to good effect.

I first got to know Peter well some time after I had retired from the game, when I was invited by MCC to be player-manager on a tour to the Leeward Islands in the West Indies. This was just about as good as it could possibly get – a four-week holiday during February in the sunshine and warmth of the Caribbean. As we travelled from island to island I quickly realised that, along with one or two others, Peter was the life and soul of the party. He could be seen sitting in the back of the mini-bus during longer journeys, singing rude songs with great spirit. He enjoyed life, took his cricket seriously and allowed little to disrupt his harmony.

Although the tour was a great success – it could hardly have failed in such convivial surroundings – an unfortunate incident occurred during the one match in which I had been entrusted with the captaincy. We were playing on the tiny island of Nevis, a short boat ride from St Kitts, from where we set off early in the morning after a good party the night before. Despite some weary eyes and sore heads we were in good spirits when we came ashore.

It was a hot day. I lost the toss, and we fielded first. The Nevis innings proceeded with ominous serenity till we came to a short drinks break. This peaceful moment for recovery was disturbed by a playful water-fight which involved Bradley Donelan (Sussex), Roland Lefebvre (Somerset) and possibly others. Lefebvre flicked some water at Donelan who retaliated by aiming a kick in the direction of Lefebvre's rear. Seeking to protect himself Lefebvre thrust his hand down in the general direction of his bottom, but unfortunately it collided with Donelan's foot on its way up. The sad outcome of this collision was that Lefebvre's arm gave way from the impact and broke.

I neither heard the crack nor saw the incident but, during the next over, Moores from behind the stumps passed messages to me which related the whole sorry tale. I now had to bowl more overs than I had expected, as did Graham Cowdrey who finished up by taking six for 12, which led to our winning the match comfortably by six wickets. As Moores observed afterwards, it's not every day that a captain achieves success as a result one of his team being laid low at the hands (or, in this case, foot) of another.

The turning point in Moores' career occurred in the spring of 1997. Over a period of time the Sussex members had become restless and discontented with the workings of their main committee and its executive team. There had been rumblings on the boundary edge, and even the most refined and loyal supporters were becoming fidgety and impatient. I must say it all took me rather by surprise. I was certainly not expecting a hostile and well-planned revolt, a sort of coup d'état on the South Coast. I had spent that winter of 1996/97 fighting my own battles with the England team in Zimbabwe and New Zealand, acting as a glorified nanny to a tour party that demanded plenty of attention. I was blissfully unaware of the shenanigans being played out at Hove or their ramifications for the county's cricket.

The bomb-shell finally exploded at the Grand Hotel in Brighton, a place with a sad association with disruption, during the club's AGM when 500 or more members crammed into the hall and, with neither ceremony nor adherence to procedure, hijacked the meeting. I, as a humble member of the committee, sat at the top table and stared out upon a sea of faces most of which, up till then, had only ever shown me friendship and goodwill. Now all I could see was hostility and menace in their eyes – an angry mob, hell-bent on overturning the current regime. I was surprised there were no police on duty to ensure fair play.

But the crowd was not interested in fair play; this was a ruthless and probably illegal take-over, but effective none the less. In the past, I had never been particularly frightened by fast bowlers tearing in down the hill at Hove and peppering me with fearsome missiles, but now here I was stranded, as it were, at the crease in front of a malevolent and threatening gathering, feeling distinctly windy. I said nothing, neither was I invited to do so. In my heart and in front of those whom I still took to be my friends, I thought for a moment I might be able to defuse the atmosphere with a few words of wisdom and humour but, looking round at the angry faces intent upon destruction, I thought better of it and held my peace. The outcome of the meeting, a ragged and ruthless affair, was the overthrow of the old guard and formation of a new committee and executive.

It was all over in a matter of moments. Alan Wadey, the vice-chairman, saved the day and spared us a riot in the Grand's ballroom by making a brief conciliatory speech which held things at bay. While the tired old committee slipped away quietly into the night, a new era for Sussex cricket was ushered in under Robin Marlar's chairmanship with his new chief executive Tony Pigott. At the same time Moores was confirmed as Sussex captain for 1997. The following year Chris Adams took over, with Moores as his right-hand man and head coach. In these unlikely circumstances Moores got the break he needed and was able to operate in an unstuffy atmosphere with the air cleansed by the defiant hand of revolution.

Moores' progress at Sussex and his close understanding of team and individual chemistries inevitably led him to catch the eye of the England and Wales Cricket Board who needed to replace Duncan Fletcher after his successful but, by now, exhausted tenure as England's head coach. Moores, who had himself moved on from Sussex to take charge of England's academy training programme at Loughborough, was a natural choice, despite his lack of international experience. Not only was he English, he was very much a product of England's coaching system, an appointment from within the circle.

Soon after the announcement of his succession to the job, I attended a dinner with Peter at the Grosvenor House Hotel in London. We sat at the same table and chatted about the future. He was typically enthusiastic and full of beans. "I don't wish to put a dampener on things," I said to him towards the end of the evening, "but at some stage I expect it will all end in tears. That's what usually happens. It's good, I think, that you should recognise this now rather than be too sad, surprised and disappointed later." He nodded and appeared to take it in. I can only hope that when the end came – unluckily and prematurely – these words were of some help and consolation. The way he subsequently conducted himself in the face of adversity and criticism gave a fine example to all sportsmen who find themselves unexpectedly caught on the back foot.

As a result of his behaviour and general demeanour I suppose the England job just could come round again – unlikely but not impossible. Stranger things have happened. His success with a far from outstanding side at Lancashire and his close understanding with Glen Chapple, his captain, have nudged him gently back into the forefront of things. He will have learnt much from Andy Flower, his successor, whom he himself appointed as his England batting coach. Flower was, of course, an exceptional batsman and wicket-keeper himself for Zimbabwe, always up against it, one who played his cricket for ever as an underdog. His tough exterior has been shaped by Zimbabwe's oppressive regime.

Moores, like Flower, has based his success on hard times. Members of Parliament, who have experienced time in opposition and with their backs to the wall, invariably have more to offer when they come to power. It's much the same in cricket.

The quality of coaching and influence of sophisticated training programmes now prepare players more thoroughly than ever before. While coaching has become increasingly scientific and technical, Moores has managed to achieve a balance which respects human nature and its frailties while constantly pushing at the boundaries of progress. The building of a team, often with an emphasis on individuality, still remains the constant and most important role of the coach within the contemporary game. Not many have been better able to work with captains, whose goals are usually set for the short term, more assuredly than Moores who as coach has always had the bigger picture in his sights. I have a feeling his best days are yet to come.

Isaac Vivian Alexander Richards

Born: St John's, Antigua, 7 March 1952

121 Tests for West Indies (1974-1991)
8,540 runs at an average of 50.23, 24 centuries
50 Tests as captain

507 first-class matches (1972-1993)
36,212 runs at an average of 49.40, 114 centuries
223 wickets at an average of 45.15

Viv Richards was voted by a panel of 100 experts one of Wisden's Five Cricketers of the Twentieth Century – alongside Donald Bradman, Gary Sobers, Jack Hobbs and Shane Warne.

Not only did Richards score great quantities of runs – the only West Indian to hit 100 first-class hundreds – he scored them with ferocious, domineering power. In 1987, on his home island Antigua, he hit the England bowlers for the fastest century in terms of balls faced, 56, in Test history.

He came to England in 1973, a shy young man who spent a year at the Lansdown club in Bath while qualifying for Somerset. Three years later he was scoring 1,710 Test runs in the calendar year, a record that stood for 30 years.

He hit a majestic century in the 1979 World Cup final. Then in 1984, at Old Trafford, he played what many consider the greatest of all one-day innings, scoring 189*, the last 93 of which were plundered after the fall of the ninth wicket.

Alongside his great friend Ian Botham he was a key member of the Somerset side which won five one-day trophies between 1979 and 1983.

Viv Richards

It was 1974. Richards had not been batting long. I was standing at slip. Snow was bowling. I suppose we had just about heard of Richards, but the slender young Antiguan was hardly a household name at this stage. It was a cold May day at Hove. Snow pounded in and banged the ball down just short of a length around the leg stump. Richards swayed elegantly onto the back foot and then, seemingly without effort, thumped the ball high over mid-on onto the top of the Gilligan stand to the south of the ground. It was a mighty blow by any standards and I might, from slip, even have been forgiven for breaking into applause but for the possibility of catching Snow's eye. It was the most accomplished and breathtaking shot I had ever seen and signalled the arrival of a very special talent.

Without a shadow of a doubt Richards was the most dominant, emphatic and indeed most daring batsman of his generation. With either his maroon West Indian or navy blue Somerset cap on his head (never a helmet) he laid waste all who stood in his way and was better able than any I can remember to change the course of a match. Just before him Sobers and Kanhai played in the same rich vein while, of his own contemporaries, Zaheer Abbas and Sunil Gavaskar might indeed have proved harder to get out, but neither were so destructive or impossible to bowl at. Possibly Javed Miandad was close to being in the same league, but his genius was rather more Baroque inspired as opposed to Richards' Wagnerian thunder. Richards would tend to hit you out of the bowling attack before you had even had time to have a bad day. It was the sheer thudding power that was so intimidating.

Few bowlers got away from Richards without at some stage receiving a fearful thrashing. I was no exception. My moment of horror came late on in my career when Sussex and Somerset were both vying for the John Player Sunday League Trophy. It was early September 1985, and a hot day; a large excited crowd had crammed into the little Taunton ground, and the stage was set. No one could afford to slip up in the crucial run-in. Despite a fine partnership between Colin Wells and Imran we never really got into our stride with the bat, and 184 runs was unlikely to baffle a powerful Somerset line-up. For all that, we struck early with a wicket and indeed felt quite relaxed as Roebuck and Popplewell began to build a sizeable partnership. But then disaster struck – a mix-up and Roebuck was run out, just when we were keeping a measure of control on proceedings.

Enter Richards. I was acutely aware that I had to change the bowling so I pottered over to Imran to ask his advice. His answer surprised me: "Viv can be a bit vulnerable against spin early on," he said, "I think you should have a go." And so I did. I wiped the sweat from my brow and set the field. I fail now to remember the exact sequence of events, but it went roughly like this. First ball Richards stepped away and clouted it over extra-cover into the pavilion for six. Second ball, he did the same but thankfully it dropped short of the boundary for four. Third ball was a mighty blow back over my head, over the perimeter wall and into the River Tone from where it was retrieved by a startled fisherman and lobbed, very wet, back onto the ground.

Fourth ball was a good one, and Viv just tapped it back to me while he took a rest. Fifth ball only conceded four so I was quite pleased to have dragged things back a bit in my favour. Sixth ball was unlucky, it flew high to deep mid-wicket where Phillipson clasped at it but the ball, still slippery from the river, eluded his grasp. Not only did he drop the ball, but it slid over the boundary for another six. Twenty-six runs came from the over and I fear that this cost us the title which, up till then, we had so richly deserved. It was a mean assault and one for which Imran must take his fair share of responsibility.

My goodness, it was hard to know how to tackle Richards. He drew people into the game – the crowd, his own team and even the opposition. We all somehow played along with him, captured by his colossal aura of muscular confidence. I tried all sorts of tactics, but on his day it was impossible to set a field that could even hold him at bay. I tried lesser bowlers in the hope he would lose concentration, saving my big guns – Imran and Le Roux – for when the wheels were really falling off. I would set an off-side field – deep cover, long-off – and instruct the bowlers to direct their attention to well wide of the off stump. I would stand alone at slip full of hope and misplaced optimism. And yet he would still porridge the ball through the leg-side with speed of eye and foot that would have made him a natural contender for *Strictly Come Dancing*. A really good bowler like Geoff Arnold, the best seamer I knew, might just force an error as he nibbled the ball about more than most. Somewhere along the line he might have got him but, if he did, I don't remember it.

One day in 1983 an extraordinary thing happened. Late in May Sussex travelled to Taunton to play Somerset in the County Championship. Richards, Botham and Garner were all playing in a Somerset team bristling with aggression and menace. But we were a match for them this time and at our best, scoring 408 for six declared in our first innings. Somerset in reply, on a spinning pitch, collapsed for 224 and followed on. I was very happy but for one thing. During Somerset's innings I had bowled a short ball (a long hop) to Peter Denning who, despite being a good friend of mine and son of the butcher in Chewton Mendip, crashed the ball directly into the knee of Chris Waller, fielding at silly point. He was felled by this hammer blow and quite clearly out of it so far as this match was concerned. He was carried off. I was left to mastermind the spin attack on my own. All was well as Somerset began its second innings, but the cloud of Richards hung heavily over us. He had failed in his first innings and would surely be keen to make amends.

With only twenty minutes of the second day remaining Roebuck missed a straight ball from Pigott and down the steps of the pavilion strode Richards, flexing his muscles and overdoing the swagger. With a few swishes this way and that he scored 30 runs. The day was over. I knew I was destined to spend the night in the County Hotel fretting over field placings and agonising about Richards' ability to spoil the final day. He kept me up all night as I littered my fielders about the floor of my room, knowing full well that I no longer had Waller to help me out in the spin department. It was a withering experience.

The new day dawned bright and sunny. I walked to the ground past St Mary Magdalene church and then the smaller St James, my mind in a whirl. With whom should I open the bowling – spin or pace? – what a worry. At 10.45am in the dressing room I sat the team down for our usual pre-match chat. "Who should bowl first?" I asked. All fingers pointed uncompromisingly at me. Opinion was unanimous. I had caused Waller's injury so I should now take up the mantle. There seemed to be little doubt about that. I was not confident, nervous in fact and intimidated by the mighty presence of Richards looming dangerously with 30 runs already to his name and warming up in the dressing room next door.

The bell rang. Out we trooped onto the field. I warmed up, ready to bowl the first over of the day with the church spires behind me and a short boundary too. I set the field; I had after all been practising all night. Two catchers in close, brave men, indeed placed so as not to give Richards a feeling of superiority, and the rest spread out mostly around the boundary. Silence as I prepared to bowl.

The ball felt clammy in my hand as I trotted in past the umpire and let it go, intending to impart a little spin on the way. The ball, in fact, slipped out of my hand a bit higher than I intended, a little more loop than necessary, but it lured Richards out of his ground as he viewed this gentle offering with keen anticipation.

He advanced and, as was his custom, he whipped his bat across the flight and, instead of stroking the ball calmly to mid-wicket, played over it whereupon it proceeded slowly towards Ian Gould, the wicket-keeper, who would have completed the stumping had not the ball, as if by a miracle, collided with the middle stump first. For a moment I stood there in shock; I thought I was dead and perhaps in heaven. Richards, bowled first ball of the day. Then I became aware of Le Roux pounding across the ground from deep square leg, ecstatic in his delight. "That's the equivalent," he said, "of catching a 20lb salmon first cast." "Better than that," I replied. Somerset never really recovered from this extraordinary turn of events and slid to defeat quite tamely, deprived as they were of the direction of their master-player.

Delving back into the past from that joyous morning at Taunton and to the early days indeed, Sussex and Somerset had crossed swords in the 1978 Gillette Cup final. This was only two years after Richards had taken the country by storm during the drought of 1976, when the West Indies had swept all aside and Richards' star shone as few have ever done before. I too had been making gentle progress and *Wisden* was moved to write that 'Barclay, on the spinning front, had strengthened his claim to be considered a useful all-rounder.' Such praise, though a little tepid, should not be sneezed at.

Anyway it was a hot day for the final at Lord's. Somerset with Richards, Garner and Botham were firm favourites and, with 14 runs coming from Imran's first over, justified the bookies' confidence. But it seemed that Somerset peaked too early – slowly and unexpectedly nerves set in. Not even Richards and Botham were quite their usual selves and seemed loath to take risks against my gentle off-spin. And then it happened. With the match delicately poised I bowled a poor ball down the leg side; Richards went for the sweep but not one of the full-blooded affairs we were used to, more of a half-baked paddle. The ball flew up off the top edge towards deep square-leg where Arnold on the boundary pouched the catch in his large safe hands. The crowd roared, mostly out of disappointment; after all, they had come to watch Richards bat, not me bowl. The Sussex team wanted to hug and kiss me but I would have none of that sort of thing and shrugged them off. I can only assume that it was this slender evidence which persuaded Imran, years later at Taunton, to convince me that Richards had a weakness against spin. From that point on Sussex clambered into the driving seat and never relinquished control. How consoling it is to feel that even the greats make mistakes and bowlers, however modest their claims may be, should never forget that it only takes one ball to get a wicket and not necessarily a very good one.

Richards never said much when he batted. He might say "Hello" occasionally and was always polite but mostly he just banged the top of his bat handle with the palm of his hand as though the grip might be slipping over the top. He bowled a bit too but very poorly compared with his batting. His bowling could be useful in one-day cricket but rather relied upon reputation; no one much liked to attack him for fear of reprisal. As a bowler he was somewhat akin to a penguin padding about on the beach whereas, as a batsman, he resembled the penguin's majesty of movement in the sea.

Richards was the finest batman against whom I ever played.

Victor Henry Douglas Cannings

Born: Bighton, Hampshire, 3 April 1919

285 first-class matches (1947-1959)
927 wickets at an average of 22.73

Vic Cannings began life as a farm labourer's son in the Hampshire village of Bighton. He served in the Palestine Police during the Second World War, played 13 summers of county cricket (for Warwickshire and Hampshire), then spent 25 years as cricket professional at Eton College.

A right-arm medium-pace bowler, he enjoyed the best years of his playing career with Hampshire, bowling in tandem with Derek Shackleton. Neither were quick as new-ball bowlers, but both had a relentless accuracy which frustrated many an opposition batsman. He took 100 wickets in a season four times, conceding his runs at little more than two an over.

For much of his playing career he spent his winters coaching abroad – in South Africa, Pakistan, the Argentine and Trinidad – and such was his reputation that, when he retired from cricket at the age of 40, several schools sought his services.

At Eton he was always true to himself, saying just what he thought and never refining his broad Hampshire accent. As such he became an immensely popular figure in the life of the school.

Now in his nineties he still lives in a house across the fields from the College.

Vic Cannings

I passed Heathrow on my right and then eased off the M25 down the M4 on my way to Slough, not a place I would willingly choose to visit. But this time I was on a special mission. Near Slough, in fact just to the south of the motorway, lives one of my favourite people from early days at school and with whom I struck up a close and endearing friendship – Vic Cannings.

In his prime Vic had been a fast bowler with Warwickshire and Hampshire and then, for the final twenty-five years of his career, and much more relevant so far as I was concerned, Eton's professional cricket coach. For years he had lived in the same house very near but just out of range of the M4. His road, a dead-end, was called The Myrke. I knew how to get there from Eton on a bicycle across country but found myself a bit flummoxed as I got close to the target by car. I drew up alongside a stranger waiting at a bus-stop and wound down the window. "Any idea where Vic Cannings lives?" I asked politely. I suppose it was a long shot, even if he had lived nearby for over fifty years. "Vic who?" came the unpromising reply from the long-haired, bearded and bespectacled man sporting two obligatory studs above the left eyebrow. It was not a great start to the evening. Eventually I found Vic's house, just the same, and there he was resplendent in dinner jacket and all, and ready for the outing. No difference from the old days – a twinkle in the eye – although I suppose a little stiffer in the limbs but in pretty good nick for 91.

We were off to London for a very important celebration. The year was 2010. Forty years earlier the Eton cricket team had performed the double by defeating both Winchester and Harrow in the same year and, by way of a party, we, the team and Vic, were all meeting up at a small dining club in London to remind ourselves unashamedly of these triumphs. All the way to London, up the M4, Hyde Park Corner, Piccadilly and down St James' Street to our destination we talked. It was just like the many times when I visited Vic in The Bat Shop, the school's sports shop, in Eton's High Street. Hours I spent there chatting to him about cricket, his days in the game and tactics. I may have learnt little else at Eton but I did have a fine training in cricket strategy and psychology. Field placing, batting orders and how to handle people were discussed at great length. "We don't want to see players standing about the field in no-man's land, just littered about," he would say. 'The confetti field' he called it, as if the captain had chucked confetti up in the air and placed players wherever it happened to land.

I shouldn't have spent so much time in The Bat Shop; it was strictly against the school rules, but I never got caught. At the time, too, I was recovering from my first serious bout of depression which was to become such a plague later on in life. But, for now, I was on the mend. Doctors had administered various types of medicine but by far the best therapy, infinitely better than any doctor, were my visits to The Bat Shop. With a cup of coffee and sitting in front of one bar of electric fire, I was, as it were, temporarily removed from this world and transferred from gloom to happiness. Vic and I just talked about cricket, and slowly I got better.

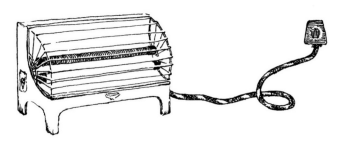

He was a great story teller, mostly true I'm sure. He would sit there, dressed in old-fashioned clothes: tweed jacket, V-necked sweater, country shirt, brown trousers, woolly cricket socks, stout brown shoes and always a tie. His bicycle and clips were parked at the back of the shop near the kettle and biscuits. The shop was very old-fashioned, nothing much on show apart from cricket bats, all Gray Nicolls – I think he must have got a good deal there – which I tried out relentlessly while we talked. Occasionally a master would pop his head in, and I would have to cower quietly in Vic's cubby-hole office. And from there the stories emanated. He talked of his time spent with the British Police in Palestine during the war. There I believe he played a lot of cricket while trying to referee the never-ending feuds between Jews and Arabs. He conceded that on the whole he had quite a good war before returning to England and the promise of county cricket, first with Warwickshire and then, much more permanently, with Hampshire.

He would talk about the old players: Peter May, the best batsman he ever saw and played against but, perhaps most of all, he talked about Derek Shackleton, 'Shack'. It was always Shack who made the ball move about before he did without ever understanding quite how he did it; he just bowled with a remarkably versatile and flexible wrist. Shack, he said, never knew the secret. Vic was convinced that, had Shack started to think, he would have been useless. And Vic's coaching style was somewhat similar. He wasn't so much a technical coach, more of a mentor and friend. Above all he made it fun, and we all laughed a lot. He teased everyone relentlessly but at the same time gave us confidence in abundance. A session in the nets or at fielding practice with Vic was never dull, and he was much loved and respected by the young players. His stature and standing as a first-rate county fast bowler – and strong – always held him in good stead.

We were nearing our destination now, looking for somewhere to park. While we were going round and round St James' Square we got back onto the subject of Shack. Or at least I did. What was interesting was the coincidence, after Vic's fruitful and happy partnership with Shack, that I too got to know him quite well years later when he joined the panel of first-class umpires. If I'm truly honest, Shack was not a great umpire – not really in the Buller, Bird and Shepherd category. The problem was that he couldn't see very well, and I think his hearing was a bit dodgy too. So he umpired by instinct, based on years of experience, and in so doing became one of my favourites. For some reason he took a liking to me. We would chat away when I was at the non-striker's end, and I don't ever remember him giving me out, especially after I became captain. I knew he knew that, at the end of the match, I marked the umpire's card. But, by contrast, he was generous to me when I bowled my off-spinners; woe betide batsmen who got hit on the pads when the ball was in my hand. I felt quite the Ray Illingworth in his prime. Sadly Shack didn't last long on the panel.

Parking a car in London can be a bugger. There are more cars and less room now, but this time I didn't much mind; it gave us more time to chat while we craned our necks this way and that for a space. We worked out that it was forty-two years since, as a 14-year-old, I had been hit on the foot by a full toss in the evening nets at Eton. I hopped about for a bit as one does but, when it came to my turn to bowl, I was struggling and making a bit of a fuss so Vic suggested I tried a few spinners off a couple of paces instead of my usual medium stuff. I did just that, and those around me were rather taken with these gentle flighted efforts (I was still quite small) and suggested I persevere with them and forget about seam and swing bowling. Indeed I did and the following Saturday, playing against Bradfield Under-14s in grey flannels and brown cricket shoes, I took six wickets and as a result was catapulted into the first XI as they had no spinner. My rise to prominence was both sudden and unexpected.

Vic never really coached me in those days. "You just bowl," he would say, "and they'll get out." I remember I wasn't so much worried by the bowling, which came quite naturally, as the people I was playing with and against – all grown-up men, deep voices, shaving and that sort of thing. Socially I was out of my depth. On the way home after matches we would often stop off at a pub for refreshments. The rest of the team were allowed to have a beer while I would sit quietly with Vic, bitter lemon in hand, as he entertained the chaps with endless stories, interrupted every now and then by references to the day's cricket – never without laughter.

At long last we found a parking space not far from the club. The ageing players were all there when we entered an old-fashioned room where drinks were being doled out. A spontaneous round of applause rang out to celebrate the arrival of a man who had meant a lot to us and done so much to help shape our lives. Vic's mind and memory could not have been sharper as he absorbed the scene and atmosphere. "Bloody hell, I never thought I'd see you lot again," he said.

Reminiscences were in full flow. He remembered Nick Boustead enjoying his tea and cakes in the barn next to the pavilion on Agar's Plough during a match when a jumbo jet, taking off from Heathrow, flew directly overhead. So loud was its noise that Boustead was moved to say, "Do you know, Vic, I hate aeroplanes." To which Vic

216

replied, "I'm not surprised, Nick, you can't eat them." On another occasion Geoff Consett, an accomplished left-hander from Yorkshire, sustained a painful blow on the inside of his knee when batting. He collapsed to the ground, writhing in agony. Vic strode out to the crease to sort things out and simply picked him up and, amidst much mirth, piggy-backed him off the field and back to the pavilion.

There was much more besides when dinner was served. There the banter rose in a crescendo till everyone was talking at once. I tried to make a speech but was drowned out by the noise before I had even managed a sentence. Vic loved it. "You're the worst bloody cricketers I've ever seen," he said, but we knew he didn't really mean it – I think. We were reminded of his signals from the boundary when we were in the field: a hand up in the air meant Henry Wyndham, who was very tall, should bowl: a foot in the air, which caused him to slip down the bank at Marlborough once, meant bring in another short-leg. There were many others too, but I've forgotten them in the course of time.

There was much talk inevitably about both Harrow and Winchester matches, two-day affairs in those days. Winchester we thrashed by an innings at Eton during which I broke my nose when fielding at first slip and diving into a catch which collided with my nose instead of my hands. The Harrow encounter was unusual for, rather than being played at Lord's, it had to be rearranged at Harrow due to the upheavals caused by the aborted South African tour in 1970. It was a much closer game, and we only just won it with six minutes to spare at the end and largely due to bowling some 26 overs in the last hour. There was much rejoicing as you can imagine. Vic, who kept his distance on such occasions and faded a little into the background, was quietly very proud. His style, humour and beaming smile played a big part in our success. He was just about the least judgemental man I have ever known.

My great friend Henry Wyndham, whose medium-pace bowling played such a large part in completing the Harrow and Winchester double, said to me years later, "I'm not really sure Vic actually taught me anything."

"I think that's the whole point, Henry," I replied.

Michael Colin Cowdrey

Born: Bangalore, India, 24 December 1932
Died: Angmering Park, Sussex, 4 December 2000

114 Tests for England (1954-1975)

7,624 runs at an average of 44.06, 22 centuries
120 catches
27 Tests as captain

692 first-class matches (1950-1976)

42,719 runs at an average of 42.89, 107 centuries

Colin Cowdrey was the first cricketer to play 100 Tests, marking the occasion in July 1968 with a century against Australia at Edgbaston. In that innings he became only the second batsman, after Wally Hammond, to score 7,000 Test runs. A fine slip fielder, he had in the previous match passed Hammond's record of 110 Test catches.

He captained Kent from 1957 to 1971, taking them from perennial also-rans to a formidable side which won the Gillette Cup in 1967 and the Championship in 1970. Yet with England he came and went as captain several times, only establishing himself in 1968. Then early the following summer he ruptured an Achilles tendon, and he never led England again. His tour of Australia in 1970/71 was his fourth as vice-captain, each time under a different man.

He served as Chairman of the International Cricket Council from 1989 to 1993. In 1997 he was given a peerage for services to the game, taking the title of Baron Cowdrey of Tonbridge. After his death in 2000 he became only the second cricketer, after Sir Frank Worrell, to be granted a memorial service in Westminster Abbey.

In 2001, in his memory, MCC inaugurated an annual Spirit of Cricket lecture.

Colin Cowdrey

Westminster Abbey on a cheerless, cold March day in 2001 formed the backdrop for Colin's memorial service, or service of thanksgiving as it is now more popularly known. It was a rousing, stimulating occasion with much humour and charm to capture the essence of Colin's gentle nature. The Abbey was full to bursting, choc-a-bloc, standing room only at the back. This was hardly surprising for Colin in his lifetime was a most popular and well-respected man and one whose legacy will live on long after his death. The music was rich in variety: Elgar's *Nimrod* to settle the nerves before the service and Widor's exciting *Toccata* at the end to hurry the congregation back out into the cool spring air. David Sheppard, himself not well at the time, said the prayers, and both John Major and Christopher Cowdrey gave addresses which encapsulated the flavour of a great friend and father with words of profundity and wit. I felt that the deeply spiritual and sometimes insecure nature of Colin was embodied in this service, the like of which I had not attended before.

Over fifteen or more years Colin became one of my greatest friends. Although I had played cricket for Sussex for more than sixteen years, I knew very few famous people other than to bowl at them occasionally and so discover quite quickly why they were famous. But with Colin he was well known not only as an outstanding cricketer but also as a statesman whose influence in both cricket and peacemaking was widely acknowledged. He didn't get knighted and then enter the House of Lords for nothing.

Our friendship and, I suppose, mutual understanding did not happen overnight. No, it was not until the Arundel Castle Cricket Foundation was formed in 1986 that we became more close, united by a scheme that would change the nature of Arundel's cricket and give opportunities to young and disadvantaged people from London and inner city areas nationwide. Amidst Colin's international and national responsibilities this was more of a challenge on home territory; it meant as much to him as anything. And I was asked to run it.

The spirit of Cowdrey came into my life much earlier than this. As a young boy it wasn't Cowdrey who was my great hero but Ted Dexter. For a start Dexter played for Sussex, my home county, and was just about the most flamboyant batsman in the country at the time, and he bowled quite fast too. Cowdrey played for Kent, and that did not endear him to me as much. His Mozartian elegance and style did not appeal to me as vividly as Dexter's Beethovenesque pomp and grandeur. My passion for cricket really sparked into life in 1963 when the West Indies visited England and competed, for me, in one of the greatest series ever. Dexter's innings of 70 in the second Test match at Lord's will be remembered by all those who saw it and many who did not – but in the same match Cowdrey, when batting well in the second innings, had his arm broken by a fearsome delivery from Wes Hall. Heroically, at the end of the innings and to save the day, he returned to the crease, arm in plaster, to bat as non-striker while David Allen blocked out the final two balls from Hall. At the time Cowdrey's heroism did not compare with Dexter's brute force and panache.

Almost unbelievably, ten years later, as a 19-year-old, I was selected early in the season to play for Sussex against Kent at Hastings. Cowdrey was still in the Kent side and batting at number four. It was a cold day in early May and Tony Greig's first match as captain. Within an hour of taking the field I was bowling at Cowdrey. For some reason I preferred in those days to bowl around the wicket, not because the ball was spinning – that was rare in my case – but just because I felt more comfortable. I was nervous, each ball something of an ordeal. Before too long I bowled an innocent, flighted half volley on Cowdrey's leg stump which he clipped politely and calmly in the air to Greig fielding at mid-wicket. Cowdrey, caught Greig bowled Barclay, 18. Just for a moment I thought I was in heaven and that cricket was an easy game. Not only that but I got a "Well bowled" from Cowdrey at lunchtime. That meant a lot. From that point on in the match my fortunes changed. Rain fell heavily overnight and the following afternoon Underwood got to work as was his custom and dismissed me first ball for 0 and the team for 67. I did a little better in the second innings when indeed I made 0 again but this time out second ball in a total of 54. I suppose on balance it was a bad game – two ducks and three balls at the crease but Cowdrey's wicket somewhat made up for Underwood's lethal bowling.

I next encountered Cowdrey, rather surprisingly, in Nigeria where we were both included in an MCC tour of West Africa. Cowdrey was on Barclays Bank business in Lagos where we were playing cricket at the time. He joined in. I made 0 in my first innings against Nigeria, and it did occur to me that at this stage in my career Cowdrey had never actually seen me score a run. Despite this he took the trouble to give me some advice. I can't for the life of me remember what he said or whether indeed it was good advice, but it was the fact that he took the trouble at all that made such a difference. In the second innings, believe it or not, I made 60 not out and we won the match. Unluckily and while I was tackling the Nigerian bowlers my traveller's cheques were stolen, a problem which, as they were in Barclays Bank's name, I might have presented to Colin. But I never had the courage to ask and, knowing Colin as I do now, I am not sure he would have been much help.

Although I probably did bump into Colin from time to time over the next ten years, we would never have done much more than pass the odd friendly word to one another. Our paths didn't cross all that often. It wasn't until August 1985, during Canterbury cricket week, that the telephone rang rather unexpectedly and, if I'm being honest, somewhat inconveniently in the dressing room just five minutes before Sussex were due to take the field against Kent. "It's for you, skip," Colin Wells shouted to me amidst the din, "it's Colin Cowdrey." I was a bit startled – Colin was still fairly high on my list of heroes – and I had to pretend that it was perfectly convenient to talk and not in the least bit distracting from the matter in hand. That was a lie.

"I've got an idea," said Colin. "Would you be at all interested in helping to set up a charitable foundation based at Arundel Castle with the intention of helping young people and their development?" It was a big question. I gulped and had a sip of coffee before replying. "Yes, of course, I'd be very interested, I'd like to hear more." "Not now," he said "you've got to go out and field. Good luck. We'll chat soon." My father, years earlier, had always taught me to say "Yes, I'm interested" to any proposition. To be interested, he said, was not a commitment, just a process of keeping the conversation going. Funnily enough we won that match at Canterbury from where we drove on to Colchester and almost beat Essex, too.

'Soon' is an interesting word. It can mean anything but in Cowdrey's case it meant Boxing Day that same year, some four months later, by which time I had more or less forgotten about our conversation at Canterbury. This time the telephone rang at home in Brighton. I answered it standing amidst wrapping paper and toys and all the rigmarole that goes with Christmas. "Would you like to come over for tea on Saturday?" Colin said, "Roger Gibbs is coming too and we can discuss our plans. Bring Mary-Lou and Georgina as well." So a plan was made, a slightly unusual one. It was very much stepping into the unknown.

Colin lived with his wife Anne in a large recently built house near Angmering on the South Downs, a few miles to the north of Worthing. We all had tea together while Georgie ran about the place excitedly. Afterwards, Colin and Roger began to fill me in with the main gist of the plans. They were both passionately keen to keep cricket going at Arundel but, at the same time, were pretty sure that the original club, set up by Lavinia, Duchess of Norfolk in memory of her husband Bernard, could not withstand the pressure on its own. And so they had come up with the idea, a rather brilliant one, of forming a charity to run alongside the existing club. The charity would have as its main objective the education of the young with a special emphasis upon the disadvantaged and disabled. At the time this was pretty pertinent stuff: teachers threatening industrial action and school sports at a low ebb with the sale of playing fields becoming commonplace. At the heart of this new project would be the social, educational and health advantages to young people from the more deprived parts of the country making visits to Arundel.

By this stage I was very interested. This sounded just my sort of thing and something new to get my head around when Sussex cricket came to a close. The charity commissioners were easily persuaded by this ambitious concept, and it took only a few weeks for charitable status to be confirmed. This was the first very positive green light. The second was that Paul Getty was keen to make a major contribution to the newly formed Foundation and this would effectively get the show on the road and enable us to build an indoor cricket school to accompany the already world-famous ground. These two priceless assets have formed the heart of our activities ever since and given thousands of young people enormous pleasure. Both Cowdrey and Gibbs were thrilled by such quick progress and the two of them, together with three more trustees, continued to open doors and create a framework from which both Club and Foundation have thrived ever since. I took very little persuading to join this small team as director of the charity and help set the ball in motion, and am still going strong some twenty- seven years later; perhaps more of a mission, a vocation, than a proper job but with an outcome I can witness at first hand. I am indebted to the original trustees and those who have followed since for giving me the chance to open up the Arundel ground to many young and deserving people.

It was Cowdrey's style and finesse that, above all things, fascinated me. Whereas, on the field, he was a man of grace and poise with a bat in his hand, off it and at home he was quite different. I remember him most clearly as a man always welcoming me warmly on the doorstep prior to our cricket chats at Angmering Park. He would be dressed in scruffy old brown corduroy trousers, slightly ill-fitting with turn-ups at the bottom, a country shirt, green cardigan well aerated with holes and worn-out bedroom slippers. Never was he happier than when clothed informally, with neither pomp nor show. This was a house where the dogs, mainly spaniels, ruled the roost and laid down the rules. Humans played second fiddle. Colin's guests, whoever they were – from the high and mighty to the gardening assistant – would be instantly put at ease by the smell of dogs and, most especially, by the muddle which Colin's study presented.

I came to love this room. A cup of coffee in hand, I would sit in an old armchair and absorb the chaos of a busy man with fingers in many pies. Files were piled up high, willy-nilly, and everywhere. Papers were strewn about the floor, books in the shelves, a whole set of *Wisdens* and other cricket books galore. The telephone would ring from time to time, and he would search for it beneath the mess. The fire would be lit in winter; a television sat on the side to give us a glimpse of the outside world. The dogs would clamber about all over him, never really helping the cause but much loved and spoilt above all else. I would give anything to have a room like this, out of bounds to cleaners and tidiers. Colin never went in for smart briefcases with which to carry his homework about, smart anything for that matter. He stuffed all his work into an ungainly sports hold-all which served as a carrier bag for all his meetings.

It was an atmosphere which provided a subtle, if old-fashioned, accompaniment to Colin's way of exerting his influence upon people. His ends were always achieved by amiable stealth, never brute force. And in this he was very successful.

His unorthodox demeanour didn't end with his old-fashioned dress sense. The dogs would frequently travel in the car and leap all over him while he drove himself about, friendly companions who made up for any lack of seat belt. And that wasn't all. His tactics during meetings were unusual in that he would spend much of the time slumped a little backwards, head cocked up slightly with his eyes peacefully shut. It was a deceptive pose, and hard it was at times to tell whether he was actually asleep or not. It kept people on their toes. Every now and then his eyes, small and dark, would open – a profound comment or two – and then more pretence of slumber. Whatever else, it would have been a mistake to underestimate Colin at a meeting.

It has been said by some that Colin lacked that cutting-edge when it came to decision making. It is true that he hated to disappoint people and wanted everyone to be his friend. He was a brilliant communicator, spent half his life on the telephone with his voice fading at the end of each conversation to indicate he must move on, sent endless notes to all his friends – short and witty – and he was a great believer in consultation. A row, or even the suggestion of a row, would make him feel sick and, if he possibly could, he would turn his back on it. Had he lived a generation earlier, I fancy he would have gone with Chamberlain's appeasement policies (as would many others) in the face of the Nazi threat. I don't think Churchill would have been his cup of tea nor would Colin, despite his bravery, have been quite the man to mastermind a war.

In reality Colin was more of a fixer than a warrior. He was something of a planner and manipulator behind the battle lines. I remember my father once telling me he had a very great friend, Leslie Glass who, as High Commissioner to Nigeria around 1969, was significantly instrumental in helping to bring to an end the war in Biafra. Apparently, he simply bumbled around in a shabby old ill-fitting suit, too warm for the climate, and plimsolls and brought all the main protagonists and chieftains together in a spirit where confrontation gradually dispersed and was replaced with good sense. Fences were mended, and the intense suffering and starvation of Biafran children diminished. Colin was not dissimilar in some ways to Glass though he possibly lacked his intellectual capacity, as did most, and I would guess that Dexter, Marlar and Sheppard were all ahead of him on that score too, but Colin was without doubt brilliant with people. He got them round the table whereupon his intensely endearing manner would get to work.

Aware of his powers of persuasion John Major, as Prime Minister, sent him in to bat in South Africa in the early 1990s when power was being delicately transferred from the ruling Nationalist Party under F.W. De Klerk to the African National Congress and its leader Nelson Mandela. Colin knew all the people and how to make the most of their talents and heal damaged egos. He helped steer and influence the tricky negotiations without actually having to be on the front line.

Colin could be pretty single-minded too when the mood took him, far from the shrinking violet some might perceive him to have been. His dithery and indecisive facade gave him good cover at times. Underestimate Colin at your peril. For example, he got his teeth into what he understood to be the true Spirit of Cricket, how the game should be played without compromising its competitive nature. He spent hours discussing with his friends all round the world how behaviour might be improved. At Test match level independent umpires and match referees were introduced, and a new code or Spirit of Cricket was added to MCC's laws of the game as a preamble. Few, if any, dissented from the initiative. Colin never flagged. He shook it about like a terrier and was determined to draft the code effectively and fluently. It had to mean something to everyone from the village green all the way to the top. Once he got a bee in his bonnet he did not easily let it go.

If Colin will be remembered for ever as a stylish batsman with a beautiful sense of timing, I will also remember him as a writer whose words flowed from the pen as the ball did from his bat. His prose was as relaxed and easy as his appearance, and this made the drafting of the Spirit of Cricket all the more straightforward. His use of language also made him a master of the memorial service address. These were gifts, nothing more; either you've got them or you haven't.

Colin did hate to be disliked. He wanted to be everyone's friend. I confess to being rather the same, but it is a flaw nonetheless. We can't be liked by everyone; it just isn't possible nor indeed is it healthy. I think I am revealing no secret by saying that Colin really did not see eye to eye with Ray Illingworth, another man I came to know well. No shame in that. Why on earth should they like each other? They were as far apart in culture and thinking as the distant shores separated by the Pacific Ocean. Illingworth was cut-throat and ruthless, a very fine England captain but, on the other hand, he could no more have helped sort out South Africa's problems than bat left-handed. Horses for courses, I think. Colin was never a push-over. He was competitive as well – a very fine racquets player and golfer too for whom, with the minimum of practice, the ball just melted away down the fairway and all with the least possible fuss or flamboyance. His competitive instincts were well disguised by his affable and discerning manner which would leave many an opponent floundering and easy prey.

Colin's charm won him many friends and admirers the world over. I think there is little doubt that Bernard, Duke of Norfolk, rather took him under his wing when he was manager of the MCC touring party to Australia in 1962/3 under Ted Dexter's captaincy. Some said the Duke almost saw Colin as the son he never had. Who knows? Doubtless Colin, with his combined charm and cricketing style, would have found himself mixing with rich, influential and famous people as well as Jim Swanton's circle of friends. It must have been hard for him to keep his eye on the ball.

Colin was a superb communicator, a fine negotiator, and once he had made up his mind about an issue would really get his teeth into things. As chairman of the International Cricket Council he brought the whole world of cricket to Lord's and enabled them to debate the affairs of a game he deeply loved. In the modern jargon he was a great facilitator but a little too sensitive and unsure of himself to put detailed plans into action. "A lovely chap, but not quite strong enough when it came to the crunch," I heard it said.

He would have made a good teacher but perhaps without the necessary authority to become a headmaster; a perceptive cricket coach too, always intrigued by the new techniques and developments in the game and never short of enthusiasm and encouragement.

And yet as a player he had doubts – not unlike Mr Prendergast in Evelyn Waugh's *Decline and Fall*. The doubts caused him at times to rein in his talent and become bogged down and becalmed, especially when batting.

But, above all else, he loved the game with a passion and never tired of its subtle twists and turns. He awoke in the morning thinking about cricket, and it was still close to him when he went to bed at night, not something that could be said about many of his illustrious contemporaries. It was an all-consuming love affair which never flagged and right up to his death was still going strong.

He was a wonderful friend to so many people, not only in the world of cricket but also far beyond it as well. For this he will be remembered most fondly.

Robert

Born: Shipley, West Sussex, 29 November 2008

Robert, a familiar presence at the Arundel Castle cricket ground, is John's dog.

Robert

Robert has become an important member of the staff at Arundel. The children who visit us from all over the country love him, mainly because he is very naughty. He eats their picnics and, I am ashamed to say, he is a thief. He tackles the waste-paper bins with gusto and is particularly severe in our groundsmen's shed where the contents are strewn haphazardly all over the floor. He leaves behind him a trail of destruction. He lingers hopefully around the dining room at lunchtime and, given half a chance, will invade the kitchen from where he is chased out by our long-suffering caterers. As I say, he is a very naughty, greedy and disobedient dog but much loved by all who visit Arundel.

Despite his lack of training he is tolerated in the office by Joe and Vanessa who find him endearing, even if they are irritated at times by muddy paws and uncouth behaviour. Robert has few dislikes but one of them is Redford who belongs to Alan Wadey, our chairman, and his wife Georgie. Redford is a beautiful long-haired dachshund and Robert, who has delusions of grandeur himself, is a Sporting Lucas terrier. Both believe the office belongs to them, and there have already been several stand-offs to disrupt the peaceful routine of administration.

Robert himself is a man of routine at home. While the kettle boils in the morning he is let outside for a brief patrol of the garden which includes a girlie squat on the lawn, his first important duty of the day. This is followed by much cosseting and doggy attention upstairs in bed from my wife, Renira, while we enjoy an early mug of tea. Breakfast television brings us the day's news while Robert cosies in and returns to sleep, unconcerned by world events.

He chases everything. There is nothing disciplined about his life. Cars and bicycles are his favourites; runners too he will have a go at, disrupting their rhythm and yapping at their legs. He is no respecter of our chickens either, and on one dark occasion came trotting proudly into the kitchen with Sir Cliff, a much-treasured, black-and-white Polish bantam hen, in his mouth. We tried to revive her, but sadly she died of shock. It was a low moment, and she was buried in the garden.

Robert loves balls. Coloured ones are his favourites, but tennis balls do nicely too. The youngsters at Arundel, many of them on a day out from London, amuse themselves for hours by throwing balls for Robert to fetch – a good game. A less good game is when he rushes onto the field of play and, without shame, snatches the match ball from some unsuspecting fielder and makes off with it. The chase is a favourite form of entertainment.

Despite his insubordinate and ill-disciplined nature he really does have a positive effect upon our ground at Arundel, which hundreds of inner-city children, many with disabilities, visit. Almost all of them love animals – the horses in our paddock especially – and this empathy has become a valuable feature of our programme. Those who have visited us in the past always ask after Robert. He makes a difference to them.

Now Robert may not be Redford's greatest friend, but nothing compares with his hatred of our cat, Myrtle. Let's face it, Robert doesn't care for cats, chases them like everything else. The cat is partly to blame. She unwisely attacked our older terrier, Comet (now no longer with us), and, as a result, was banned to the pantry, washing machines and all. Needless to say Robert and Myrtle have from time to time met, a head-on clash, fur flying and filthy noise. On one occasion when I was cooking dinner for Renira (a rare occurrence) and just in the process of dishing up – never easy – suddenly there was a fearful set-to in the kitchen. Amidst the steaming vegetables I had to rescue the cat from the jaws of Robert who had pounced upon her. It was a close-run thing; I saved the cat and, despite the scars of battle on my hands, served dinner. We all, I am pleased to say, survived to see another day.

When in peaceful and submissive mood, Robert likes to sit on my desk in the office, eyeing up the assortment of balls deposited there. From time to time he will wander about so as to get a better view out of the window and in so doing frequently treads on the keys of my new lap-top. Actually, if I'm honest, I came to the world of new technology late in life and this is my first lap-top which I am, with the help of Vanessa, slowly learning to master. Robert's journeys around my desk and onto the lap-top have not been helpful to the cause and at times make me short-tempered, but he does at least get a good view of the action through the window.

Call us biased, but Renira and I think Robert is a very handsome dog, part Sealyham and part Norfolk, I believe, brown and white and made of wool, not hair. He has very long eyelashes which I am sure would woo the girls, were he able to do so. He does though have a very good tail to make up for his deprivation in the trouser department. Admittedly he does occasionally forget himself and get a bit gay with other dogs, particularly his best friend Trumpet when he comes to stay. Neither seem too concerned, and I think it's really all part of a doggy platonic friendship – sort of.

Robert, like most dogs, loves to be taken for a long walk; never is he happier than when chasing squirrels, rabbits, pheasants or deer. Although he rarely catches anything, his enthusiasm is undiminished and it exercises him well. He even has a fetish for pants which he extracts from our laundry basket without embarrassment, often shaking them into submission. Once in the wildest and most remote part of Scotland Renira had to extract from his mouth a rather nasty, unclean pair, retrieved from beneath a boat moored on dry land beside a bothy. They had clearly been abandoned, being beyond redemption. Their discovery didn't sit well with our picnic lunch amidst the snow-capped mountains.

More recently he has become a fine fishing companion too. Near to where we live is a lake full of carp. I've taken to fishing for them with my fly rod and line and a hook baited with bread crust. The tactics work surprisingly well. I float the bread around in the margins while Robert is alert to every movement. Now and then I catch one, a big one sometimes, and all hell lets loose in the pond – much thrashing and dashing, ducking and weaving – and rod bending double. Robert can't contain himself. It's something else for him to chase. In he jumps, paddling away successfully with his paws, and eventually I have to retrieve first the dog and then the fish in the landing net. Robert is very pleased with the catch and proceeds to lick the poor fish while I proudly take photographs. Astonishingly the fish seems none the worse for this ghastly ordeal – hook in the mouth and all – which must have interrupted a peaceful afternoon. Robert and I return to the bank where he tries to devour

234

as much of the bait as possible. We sit there in harmony, together surveying the scene and keeping a watchful eye on the ducks.

He does love water, so do I. Every month we visit Stockbridge in Hampshire together, and there we meet up with Stephen Chalke to discuss this book and much else besides. Stephen and I spend some three happy hours together in the Grosvenor Hotel, chatting about cricket mainly and having lunch too. Afterwards Robert and I go for a walk along the River Test. The water is clear, and he jumps in and swims. He chases the coots and ducks but is more wary about swans who hiss threateningly at him. Water rats are his favourites as well as the fish, who are not impartial to the odd dog biscuit and swirl about impressively. There are plenty of other dogs on the bank for company and much sniffing goes on.

It is fitting that this book should reach its conclusion in Stockbridge for it is there that Stephen and I have shaped its contents. All sorts of ideas have emerged by just chatting away, and all in a place very dear to our hearts; the wide high street, country shops and the river running through it with large trout on show never fail to raise our spirits. The pleasure of writing is not so much in how many books might be sold but rather more in the hours of preparation, contemplation and reflection that help produce the finished article which this now is.

Index